D1738523

Banned!

ALSO BY DONALD J. ROGERS

Press versus Government: Constitutional Issues

Banned!

Book Censorship in the Schools

Donald J. Rogers

JULIAN MESSNER  NEW YORK

Copyright © 1988 by Donald J. Rogers

Published by Julian Messner,
A Division of Simon & Schuster, Inc.
Simon & Schuster Building
Rockefeller Center
1230 Avenue of the Americas
New York, NY 10020

JULIAN MESSNER and colophon are trademarks
of Simon & Schuster, Inc.

Manufactured in the United States of America

10 9 8 7 6 5 4 3 2

Library of Congress Cataloging in Publication Data

Rogers, Donald J.
   Banned! : Book Censorship in the Schools.

   Bibliography: p.
   Includes index.
   1. Censorship—United States. 2. Children's
literature—Censorship. 3. School libraries—United
States—Censorship. 4. Text-books—United States—
Censorship. I. Title.
Z658.U5R64   1988   025.2′1878′0973   87-7736

ISBN 0-671-63708-8

Contents

Banned!

Introduction

When things were at their worst, about eight thousand students stayed away from school. More than four thousand miners walked off their jobs. Picketers closed bus stations, grocery stores, and building sites. A car was fire bombed. Two buses were hit by shotgun blasts. Three gasoline-filled beer bottles were thrown at an elementary school. One man was shot and another severely beaten. A local minister asked protesters to pray that three school board members would die.

What was the reason for all this violence? Was it because of disagreements between mine workers and mine owners? Was it because of tensions between blacks and whites? Although labor problems and racial conflicts both played parts in this drama, the main argument was over *books.* In 1974 Kanawha County, West Virginia, became the site of one of the most emotional school book battles America has ever seen.

1

The question in Kanawha County was whether students should be allowed to read books to which some citizens objected. Very simply, the issue was *censorship*. Censorship is the attempt by some people to limit what other people may read, write, say, hear, or see. Censors usually feel that they are protecting others from harmful or dangerous ideas.

All societies have people who would like to censor ideas. In a dictatorship the government tries to keep citizens from discussing ideas that it feels threaten political leaders. In a democracy private groups may organize to fight ideas that they feel threaten their basic beliefs. For example, in the March 1982 issue of *Censorship News*, Robert Billings stated that, censorship has become a necessity because sick educators have felt that presenting life in the raw produced a better student than the tried and true methods of a few generations ago . . . with their emphasis on right and wrong, honesty and striving for perfection.

Unlike dictatorships, most democracies limit how far censors can go. In the United States, for example, the First Amendment to the Constitution guarantees the free flow of ideas. The amendment says: "Congress shall make no law respecting an establishment of religion, or prohibiting the free exercise thereof; or abridging the freedom of speech, or of the press; or the right of the people peaceably to assemble, and to petition the government for a redress of grievances." However, Americans often argue about what these freedoms actually mean and how they apply to individual cases.

Those who would censor textbooks and school library books generally try to do so in four ways. First, they try to pressure publishers into leaving out certain words, pictures, or information. Second, they try to stop school districts from buying "offensive" books. Third, they attempt to remove already purchased books from classrooms or libraries. Fourth, they try to limit access to already purchased books by requiring parental permission for their use.

Attempts at controlling what students may read date back to the Civil War. Before the war most textbooks were published in the North. Some Southerners objected to geography books that described the North as more important than the South. Others rejected history books that praised New England settlers as models for young people to imitate. And still others objected to discussions of the evils of slavery.

Threatened with sales losses in the South, Northern publishers began to censor themselves. They cut out passages that might offend Southerners. Sometimes they even published one version of a book for the North and a different version of the same book for the South. After the war Union and Confederate veterans tried to pressure publishers into presenting one-sided views of the conflict.

The years from 1900 to 1916 are known as the Progressive Era in American history. During this period many reformers were determined to correct problems in American society. One problem was prejudice against some ethnic and religious groups. In 1911 a citizens' committee in Meriden, Connecticut, succeeded in removing William Shakespeare's *The Merchant of Venice* from the public school curriculum. The committee felt that the play presented Jews in a bad light and encouraged hatred of the Jewish people.

After the United States helped win World War I, a wave of patriotism swept across the country. Several patriotic pressure groups tried to influence textbook content. The Veterans of Foreign Wars worked to eliminate "un-American" texts. The Hearst newspaper chain published a series of articles against "pro-British" history books. And the mayor of Chicago, William "Big Bill" Thompson, made opposition to "pro-British" books part of his third-term reelection campaign.

During the Roaring Twenties American censors had Bolshevism on their minds. In 1917 the Bolshevik party (later known as the Communist party) took control of the Russian government. Some Americans feared that European immigrants would bring Bolshevism into the United States. The Ku Klux Klan complained about books inspired by "anti-Christian Jews," Roman Catholics, and Bolsheviks. In 1921 the U.S. Commissioner of Education banned the teaching of "communism and socialism" in the public schools.

The granddaddy of all censorship cases was the Scopes "monkey trial" of 1925. The trial did not focus on a specific textbook. However, the case did raise the question of whether students should be taught an idea that many of their parents rejected. The idea was Charles Darwin's theory of evolution. This theory suggests that human beings and apes evolved or developed over a long period of time from some common ancestor.

The state of Tennessee had an anti-evolution law. It forbade the teaching of any idea that contradicted the Biblical description of creation. John T. Scopes, a high school biology teacher in Dayton, Tennessee, taught his students Darwin's theory. He was arrested and charged with violating the law.

Scopes's trial pitted the famous defense lawyer Clarence Darrow against the three-time Democratic presidential candidate William Jennings Bryan. Bryan was a fundamentalist. He believed in a strict, literal interpretation of the Bible. Despite Darrow's strong challenge to Bryan's beliefs, the defense lost the case. Scopes was found guilty of breaking the law and was fined one hundred dollars. The Tennessee Supreme Court later said that the fine was too high, but the court also said that the state law did not conflict with the First Amendment. In fact, Tennessee's anti-evolution law stayed in effect until 1967, when the state legislature repealed it.

During the thirties and forties censors in the United States attacked school books that criticized the American way of life. Between 1938 and 1942 the Advertising Federation of America, the National Association of Manufacturers, and the American Legion waged the greatest pressure group campaign ever conducted against a textbook series and its author. The series was *An Introduction to Problems of American Culture.* It included social science books for both elementary and junior high school students. The author was Harold O. Rugg, a professor of education at Columbia University.

The Advertising Federation of America charged Rugg with "attacking business from every angle," mocking "the ideas and traditions of American democracy," and "making a subtle plea for abolition of our free enterprise system and the introduction of a new social order based on the principles of collectivism." In defense of himself and his books, Rugg said: "Censor the schools and you convict yourselves by your very acts as the most subversive enemies of democracy. Censor education and you destroy understanding, . . . you instate bias, . . . you give free reign to prejudice, . . . finally you create fascism. Nothing but an education in the whole of American life will build tolerant understanding of our people and guarantee the perpetuation of democracy." Some states did censor Rugg's books; others did not.

After World War II the Cold War between the United States and the Soviet Union began. It was a period of increased tension between the two superpowers. Americans were especially worried about communist expansion into the Mediterranean area, Eastern Europe, and Korea. Senator Joseph R. McCarthy searched for communist sympathizers in the U.S. government. And would-be censors looked for communist influence in the nation's schools.

In 1953 a group of citizens asked the Texas State Textbook Commission to ban editions of Geoffrey Chaucer's *Canterbury Tales* and Herman Melville's *Moby Dick* illustrated by Rockwell Kent. Kent supposedly had "Communist connections." The group also requested the banning of some six hundred other books for similar reasons.

That same year the State Legislature of Alabama passed a new law. It said that no textbook "will be adopted . . . without a statement by the publisher or author indicating that the author . . . is not a known advocate of Communism or Marxist Socialism." Textbook publishers felt that this law was unfair. Twenty-five of them sued the Alabama State Board of Education and the Alabama State Textbook Commission. On May 10, 1954, the circuit court at Montgomery found the law unconstitutional.

During the Korean War the Chinese Communists coined a new word—"brainwashing." It referred to torture methods that Chinese and North Korean soldiers used to make American prisoners accept the communist view of things. In 1958 a book called *Brainwashing in the High Schools* by E. Merrill Root was published. Root, a college English professor, argued that the United States was losing the Cold War because American history textbooks "brainwashed" students with communist ideas. Despite criticisms of the author's methods and conclusions, the book sold fairly well.

In 1959 the National Defense Committee of the Daughters of the American Revolution started circulating a textbook study. The study named 165 "subversive" books that the DAR felt threatened the safety of the United States. The DAR list helped Governor Ross Barnett of Mississippi get the power to select all the texts for his state. Governor Barnett told publishers: "Clean up our textbooks. Our children must be properly informed of the Southern and true American way of life."

The 1960s were years of emotional, sometimes violent, conflicts between old ideas and new ideas. At the beginning of the decade, a group called Texans for America tried to stop the state textbook committee from approving several history books. The "Texans" were against books that favorably mentioned the income tax, federal aid to farms and schools, the Tennessee Valley Authority, Social Security, unemployment payments, labor unions, racial integration, General George C. Marshall, the U.S. Supreme Court, and the United Nations.

The group's president, J. Evetts Haley, even opposed presenting both sides of such topics. "The stressing of both sides of a controversy," he said, "only confuses the young and encourages them to make snap judgments based on insufficient evidence. Until they are old enough to understand both sides of a question, they should be taught only the American side."

At the same time the National Association for the Advancement of Colored People managed to have an English textbook banned from the high school in Torrington, Connecticut. The book included "The Gold Bug," "Br'er Rabbit," and "Sonny's Christening." The NAACP felt that these stories ridiculed black people. Later, other citizens—both black and white—tried to remove *The Adventures of Huckleberry Finn* from various schools across the nation. They objected to Mark Twain's use of an insulting slang word for Negro.

In 1968 the United States Supreme Court considered a case similar to the Scopes case. Susan Epperson, a high school biology teacher, objected to an Arkansas law. It was a 1929 verison of the 1925 Tennessee anti-evolution statute. In effect, the Arkansas law said that if Epperson used a textbook which included Darwin's theory of evolution, she could lose her job. The Court ruled in *Epperson* v. *Arkansas* that the law was unconstitutional because it conflicted with the First and Fourteenth Amendments. The Fourteenth Amendment says that state governments as well as the federal government must respect the rights guaranteed in the Constitution, including those of freedom of speech and of the press.

Justice Abe Fortas wrote the majority opinion in *Epperson.* He warned all would-be censors that "the First Amendment 'does not tolerate laws that cast a pall of orthodoxy over the classroom.' " Presumably, he meant that lawmakers could not legislate one official view of the truth and reject all other views. The *Epperson* case became an important precedent for later cases. A precedent is a court decision that other judges may follow if they are presented with similar facts.

Despite Fortas's warning, attempts at censoring textbooks and school library books did not end with the sixties. Some observers even think that school book battles have increased during the seventies and eighties. In a 1979 article for *Publishers Weekly,* Edward B. Jenkinson listed twenty protest groups that opposed the treatment of forty different topics in school.

The following chapters of this book describe dramatic school book battles that have occurred in the 1970s and 1980s. All these disputes have involved courtroom clashes. The cases cover a fascinating range of subjects. And for Americans who are concerned about the meaning of the First Amendment, the decisions make important reading.

Chapter 1

A Life in Spanish Harlem

Harlem, a district of New York City, is mainly a black community. But many Spanish-speaking Puerto Ricans live in the eastern part of the district in an area known as Spanish Harlem. Life in Spanish Harlem has always been tough.

Down These Mean Streets is a book about growing up in Spanish Harlem during the 1940s and 1950s. It was written by Piri Thomas, an American whose family had come from Puerto Rico, and published by Knopf in 1967. The book describes the author's life from the ages of twelve to twenty-eight.

During those sixteen years Thomas tried to deal with the prejudices that dark-skinned Puero Ricans often face in the United States. To build a "cool" reputation, he joined a gang, had sex, took drugs, committed robbery, and wounded a police officer. He spent six years in prison. Then he changed his ways and helped others avoid a life of crime. Thomas's story is told in the crude, coarse language that the author learned on the streets of Spanish Harlem.

Most reviewers warned readers about the book's language but praised its message. Morris A. Forslund, a member of the Sociology Department at the University of New Mexico, thought that readers of the book would gain a lot of insight into the problems of Puerto Ricans living in Spanish Harlem. Writing for *The World Journal Tribune*, Nelson Aldrich felt that the book was important because it described conditions under which hundreds of thousands of boys grew up. The critic for *Harper's Magazine* liked the author's honesty and his passion for life. In the *Library Journal* Valeria Gregory admitted that the book might shock some young adults but felt that it vividly described current minority group problems. And Daniel Stern in *The New York Times Book Review* cautioned against ignoring cries of pain from America's minorities.

As an example of the book's message and style, Stern quoted this passage about Thomas's run-in with a prison guard:

Okay, Jesus, here goes my parole, here I go, wash me away. Moms, is it gonna hurt much? Here lies Piri Thomas, done in at Comstock Prison by a hack dressed in blue with a big brown stick. He tried to be a war counselor again, like he always was, and he cried heart and went out with a rep, and didn't complain because he had said his piece, and after all, the law of averages was against him from the jump—oh, yeah, and this stone-hearted bopper stood his ground like a champ. . . . Now I lay me down to sleep, 'cause this hack my head will beat.

Some critics, however, questioned the value of the book's style *and* content. According to a review quoted in *Contemporary Authors*, John Clark characterized the language of *Down These Mean Streets* as vulgar and obscene. He also complained: "Certainly a prejudiced society helped to fashion the monster Thomas reveals himself to have been, but his . . . frankly filthy mind seems only incidentally related to the racial injustice upon which he casually blames all his [wrongdoings]." Clark's view of the book was a sign of trouble to come.

On March 31, 1971, Community School Board No. 25 of Queens County, New York, decided in executive session to remove the book from three junior high shcool libraries. Some school district residents objected to the author's use of four-letter words. Some disliked his detailed descriptions of sexual experiences, criminal violence, and drug addiction. But at the April 19 public meeting of the board, sixty-one out of sixty-three speakers argued for *keeping* the book on the shelves. Piri Thomas even made an appearance. He maintained: "I'm not here to defend the book. I'm here to defend the right of the truth to be said." Nevertheless, the board voted five to three in favor of removing the book from the library.

Several presidents of parent-teacher groups, seven parents or guardians, three students, two teachers, a librarian, and a junior high school principal joined together to fight the board's action. They called themselves the Presidents Council. Along with the New York Civil Liberties Union, they filed a law suit against the board.

Presumably, the council members were motivated by ideas similar to those that prompted Curtis Bok, a Pennsylvania judge and parent, to speak out in favor of two other books criticized for their controversial words and ideas. Judge Bok said:

It will be asked whether one would care to have one's young daughter read these books. I suppose that by the time she is old enough to wish to read them she will have learned the biologic facts of life and the words that go with them. . . . If the young ladies are [shocked] by what they read, they can close the book at the bottom of page one; if they read further, they will learn what is in the world and in its people, and no parents who have been [careful] with their children need fear the outcome.

The Presidents Council suit claimed that the board's decision violated the First, Fourth, Fifth, and Fourteenth Amendments to the Constitution. Among other things, the First Amendment forbids government interference with freedom of the press. The Fourth Amendment prohibits unreasonably seizing a person's property. The Fifth Amendment prevents taking a person's property "without due process of law," that is, without following the proper legal steps. And the Fourteenth Amendment says that state government officials must abide by all the other amendments. In other words, the Presidents Council asked a federal trial court to declare the banning of *Down These Mean Streets* unconstitutional. It also asked the court to order the board to put the book back on library shelves.

On June 2 the school board held a special meeting to reconsider the problem. This time the board members voted five to zero (three didn't vote) to let schools that already had the book keep it. Teachers could talk about the book in class and could assign it for out-of-class reading. But only students' *parents* could actually check the book out of the library. Meanwhile, the federal trial court judge dismissed the Presidents Council suit on the grounds that no constitutional right had been violated. But the citizens' group appealed the case to the next highest court.

Presidents Council, District 25 v. *Community School Board No. 25* was the first case to bring up an important issue. The question was whether a school board has the authority to remove a book from a school library. The council's lawyers admitted that Community School Board No. 25 had the authority to select books. But once books had been selected, the board could not *remove* them just because board members disliked the books' language or content. In fact, having a book in the library gave students a constitutional right to read it.

The council's lawyers also argued that *Down These Mean Streets* was not "dirty" or obscene according to the legal definition of obscenity. In addition, there was no evidence that the book's presence in the school library distracted students from their studies. In support of the council's position, the Authors League of America filed an *amicus curiae* brief. This is a document submitted by "friends of the court" who are not directly involved in the case but are interested in its outcome.

The school board defended its position by submitting sworn statements from principals, teachers, and psychologists who opposed the use of Thomas's work. One psychologist maintained: "If youngsters are steeped in a literature of violence, lawlessness, sexual [freedom] and [abnormality] at this time of life, it cannot but influence their development [unfavorably], no matter how significant the underlying purpose of the book."

Almost a year after the book had been banned, the United States Court of Appeals for the Second Circuit agreed with the trial court's decision that no constitutional right had been violated. Judge William H. Mulligan wrote the majority opinion. He realized why the book had been purchased—to help white, middle-class, junior high school students understand life in Spanish Harlem. But he concluded that a school board *does* have the authority to remove as well as to select books. He explained: "It would seem clear to us that books which become obsolete or irrelevant or were improperly selected initially, for whatever reason, can be removed by the same authority which was empowered to make the selection in the first place."

Judge Mulligan also thought that allowing only parents to

check out the book did not violate students' First Amendment rights. He called the harm of such a limited-access policy "miniscule." And he commented: "The . . . shouts of book burning, witch hunting and violation of academic freedom hardly elevate this . . . strife to First Amendment constitutional proportions."

Finally, the judge noted that the Presidents Council could still appeal the book's banning to city and state educational officials. Therefore, the *courts* should not review the district board's decision. Judge Mulligan used *Epperson v. Arkansas* as a precedent for this conclusion. He quoted Justice Fortas: " 'By and large, public education in our Nation is committed to the control of state and local authorities. Courts do not and cannot intervene in the resolution of conflicts which arise in the daily operation of school systems and which do not directly and sharply implicate basic constitutional values.' " Judge Mulligan added that getting the courts involved in textbook or library book decisions did not promote academic freedom.

Despite this setback the Presidents Council took the matter to the United States Supreme Court. However, on November 6, 1972, the high court refused to hear the case. Justices William O. Douglas and Potter Stewart dissented, or disagreed, with this decision. Justice Douglas gave reasons for his dissent. "The First Amendment involves not only the right to speak and publish," he said, "but also the right to hear, to learn, and to know. And this Court has recognized that this right to know is 'nowhere more vital than in our schools and universities.' "

Justice Douglas also raised some new issues: "What else can the School Board now decide it does not like? How else will its sensibilities be offended? Are we sending children to school to be educated by the norms of the School Board or are we educating our youth to shed the prejudices of the past, to explore all forms of thought, and to find solutions to our world's problems? . . . Because the issues raised here are crucial to our national life, I would hear argument in this case."

Presidents Council, District 25 v. *Community School Board No. 25* was a fairly simple but important case. It was simple because it involved one main issue and a single book. The Second Circuit Court stayed with the traditional view that judges should not meddle in school board decisions. Community School Board No. 25's decision to limit access to *Down These Mean Streets* seemed reasonable enough. There was no evidence that Piri Thomas wrote the book specifically for junior high school students. And the students could probably have learned about life in Spanish Harlem from other books that were more acceptable to their parents.

The case was important for several reasons. It supported a school board's authority to remove a book from a school library. It became a precedent for future cases. In addition, it included several elements that would appear again in later school book battles, such as disagreements over a book's value, attempts at censorship, and clashes between various citizens' groups.

Justice Douglas's dissent did not affect the outcome of this case. But it did help explain what most groups fight about in these kinds of cases. The basic conflict is over the right to know versus the need to protect.

In a democracy differences of opinion between many groups of citizens are valuable. Such differences help maintain a fair and reasonable balance between various points of view. But during any given time period, one group's way of thinking may exert more pressure than another's. Sometimes people who support the right to know decide the outcomes of most school book disputes; other times people who favor the need to protect decide the outcomes. Serious problems develop when one group's point of view becomes so powerful that it threatens the constitutional rights of others.

We can use this idea of pressure groups to analyze the cases covered in this book. In the process we can determine whether the right to know or the need to protect has received more emphasis during the 1970s and 1980s. Finally, we can draw conclusions about censorship in American education today.

In this case, the Presidents Council, the New York Civil Liberties Union, and the Authors League of America were pressure groups that supported the right to know. They felt that junior high school students in the New York City area should know more about life in Spanish Harlem. They also felt that *Down These Mean Streets* gave students a realistic view of that life. Community School Board No. 25 favored the need to protect. The board members who voted for removing or limiting access to the book felt that their students should not be exposed to dangerous ideas about sex, crime, and drugs.

Sometimes courts take compromise positions between competing pressure groups. But in *Presidents Council, District 25* v. *Community School Board No. 25*, the Second Circuit Court ruled in favor of the board. The court did not say what it thought about *Down These Mean Streets,* but it did recognize the board's authority—and therefore power—to shield students from the author's language and ideas. So the court's decision was a victory for the need to protect.

The following chapters show that other conflicts between different pressure groups were much more complicated and were much more difficult to solve. For example, if the *Presidents Council* case could be called a battle, then the conflict in Kanawha County, discussed in Chapter 2, was a full-scale war.

Chapter 2

The Kanawha County War

t might take a decade before we can understand what happened."
That's how Kenneth E. Underwood, superintendent of schools
for Kanawha County, felt after most of the violence had ended.
Now that more than a decade has passed, perhaps
it is finally possible to understand what actually did happen.

Kanawha County lies in the southwestern part of West Virginia. It includes Charleston, the state capital. Most of the people
who lived in Charleston during the 1970s had graduated from high
school, and many had also attended college. Of these city dwellers,
most worked in offices and made more money than the farmers and
miners who lived in the nearby countryside.

Most of the people who lived in rural Kanawha County had
less education than Charleston residents. But more importantly,
the mountain and valley folk had very different ideas about society

17

and religion. Their views were shaped by the fact that they were often the butt of cruel jokes and the victims of greedy coal and timber companies. One rural minister explained: "We are very [mistrustful] of what people want to do with us or to us, especially those that are in authority, because we've been put through the wringers of [dishonesty] by the courts, by the lawyers, by the Board of Education, and we just don't feel that we can [risk] any more of our [selves]."

As a result of their experiences, the rural people of Kanawha County developed a strong fundamentalist faith. Their belief in the Bible helped them cope with the hardships of life. A reporter described the basic difference between the city dwellers and the county folk as the difference "between people who depend on books and people who depend on the Book."

On March 12, 1974, the county school board held one of its regular monthly meetings. A teachers' committee presented a list of 325 language arts textbooks for the board's approval. These books were chosen from a longer list already approved by the state board of education. In 1970 the state board had set certain requirements for all texts used in West Virginia schools. The books needed to "accurately portray minority and ethnic group contributions to American growth and culture and . . . depict and illustrate the intercultural character of our pluralistic society."

On April 11 the Kanawha County School Board voted five to zero in favor of approving the 325 textbooks. But one board member, Mrs. Alice Moore, made a motion to delay buying the books until they could be examined more thoroughly. She was the wife of a local minister and the mother of three children. Mrs. Moore had been elected to the board after opposing sex education courses in 1969. She felt that most of the language arts texts "contained material that was disrespectful of authority and religion, destructive of social and cultural values, obscene, pornographic, unpatriotic, or in violation of individual and familial rights of privacy."

Mrs. Moore had been talking with Mel and Norma Gabler. The Gablers were the founders of Educational Research Analysts of Longview, Texas. The purpose of the organization was to review textbooks. The Gablers became concerned about textbook content in 1961. One of their sons had shown them his American history book. It seemed to emphasize the federal government's constitutional powers more than states' rights and individual freedom. The Gablers disagreed with this view of the Constitution and began to criticize other textbooks publicity.

The Kanawha County School Board held a special meeting on May 16 at which the teachers' committee defended its book choices. Among other things, the committee members argued that America is a pluralistic society, that is, a nation made up of many different kinds of people. Therefore, students need textbooks that expose them to different points of view and that challenge them to think. At the meeting Mrs. Moore questioned this philosophy, and after the meeting she started a strong campagin against the language arts texts in the conservative, fundamentalist churches of Kanawha County.

In late June twenty-seven ministers called the books immoral and indecent. But ten other ministers voiced their support for the texts. The Reverend James Lewis said: "The books in question are creative books written with the intention of helping our children discover the truths. . . . These books open up a world of opinion and insight. They're not un-American or ungodly."

Almost a thousand people came to the June 27 board meeting. By a vote of three to two, the board members decided to drop eight of the most controversial books. The remaining 317 texts were approved for purchase.

Throughout the summer various citizens' groups protested against the approved books. One organization called itself Christian-American Parents; another, the Concerned Citizens of Kanawha County. These groups criticized different books for different reasons. Some didn't like a collection of myths that seemed to threaten the literal understanding of the Bible. The teacher's manual for the collection suggested that students compare the myth of Androcles and the Lion with the story of Daniel in the Lions' Den. One protestor's sign read: "God is not a myth to our children."

Others thought that a book by Sigmund Freud and a poem by E. E. Cummings were dirty. As one offended woman put it: "I have a Bible. I don't need those dirty books." Many admitted that they hadn't read the material. But one demonstrator explained: "I wouldn't read that filth."

Still others feared that works by black writers like Eldridge Cleaver and Dick Gregory would stir up racial troubles. A protestor told a *Washington Post* reporter: "The relations between black and white in this country improved for a time, but now they're going down. They're trying to say all white people are your enemy."

Mrs. Moore objected to one assignment in a writing book. The instructions asked students to tell their classmates how their parents interfered in their private lives. The board member felt that this assignment forced children to criticize their elders. Even an illustrated version of *Jack and the Beanstalk* came under attack. The story seemed to imply that it was all right for poor people to rob and kill rich people.

In defense of the textbooks, a spokesman for the D. C. Heath publishing company said that about half a million children across the country were using the publisher's books without any complaints. A spokesman for Scott, Foresman and Company tried to explain the difficulty of selecting material that pleased everyone.

When school started in September, the conflict between those who approved of the newly purchased textbooks and those who didn't remained unresolved. Protesting parents kept nearly 20 percent of Kanawha County's students away from classes. Picketers carried signs that read: "When the books go out, the kids go back in." Some fundamentalist ministers suggested the opening of private Christian schools for protestors' children.

Thousands of mine workers staged sympathy strikes. Mine owners, though, had doubts about the strikers' motives. If the workers could reduce coal stockpiles, then they could force the owners to raise wages. But some miners seemed genuinely convinced of "Communist influence" in the schools.

Strong feelings between opposing groups led to violence. After several bombing and shooting incidents, Superintendent Underwood briefly closed the county's 121 schools. He also canceled extracurricular activities for a weekend.

On September 11 the school board offered a compromise. All of the new texts would be removed from the classrooms. An eighteen-member citizens' committee would review the books and make recommendations within thirty days.

Some protest leaders accepted the compromise, but others refused to go along with the idea. One fundamenatalist minister asked: "Why should we settle for one thing less than we've been hollerin' for? It's the difference between Heaven and Hell for our children." And another told a rally: "We could use a big book-burning right here."

On September 12 students at George Washington High School walked out of their classes to protest the compromise. These students saw nothing wrong with the new books they were using. A few days later Mrs. Moore charged that the citizens' review committee included too many protextbook people. And the Authors League of

America sent a telegram to President Gerald Ford challenging the whole citizens' review concept. The telegram said in part: "No groups have the right to dictate what particular books may not be used by the schools of their community. The selection of books is the professional responsibility of teachers and school administrators."

In early October Mrs. Moore invited the Gablers to speak to area residents. The couple addressed as many groups as they could during a six-day swing through the county. Violence flared up again later in the month and continued into early November.

On November 8 the school board tried once more to end the dispute. Four out of the five board members voted to return almost all of the new textbooks to the classrooms. Two series of books were placed in the school libraries. These books could be taken out only with parental permission. And Superintendent Underwood said that he would resign at the end of his term.

However, in mid-November three board members and the superintendent were served with arrest warrants. The charge was contributing to the delinquency of minors. Allegedly, the four school officials had corrupted the young people of Kanawha County by allowing them to use un-American and un-Christian textbooks.

On November 21 the board approved these seven new guidelines for textbook selection:

1. Textbooks for use in the classrooms of Kanawha County shall recognize the sanctity of the home and emphasize its importance as the basic unit of American society. Textbooks must not intrude into the privacy of students' homes by asking personal questions about inner feelings or behavior of themselves or their parents, or encourage them to criticize their parents by direct questions, statements or inferences.
2. Textbooks must not contain profanity.

3. Textbooks must respect the right of ethnic, religious or racial groups to their values and practices and not ridicule those values and practices.

4. Textbooks must not encourage or promote racial hatred.

5. Textbooks must encourage loyalty to the United States and the several states and emphasize the responsibilities of citizenship and the obligation to redress grievances through legal processes.

6. Textbooks shall teach the true history and heritage of the United States and of any other countries studied in the curriculum. Textbooks must not defame our nation's founders or misrepresent the ideals and causes for which they struggled and sacrificed.

7. Textbooks used in the study of the English language shall teach that traditional rules of grammar are a worthwhile subject for academic pursuit and are essential for effective communication among English speaking people.

The board also approved new methods for textbook selection. The board members would set up a screening committee in each subject area. Then they would appoint three parents and one teacher to each committee. Three committee votes would be needed to keep a textbook in any subject.

Teachers in the school system became concerned about the possible effects of these new guidelines and methods. So they asked the National Education Association, the nation's largest teachers' organization, to investigate the entire matter.

An NEA panel held hearings in Kanawha County from December 9 to December 11. The panel members listened to individuals and groups on both sides of the conflict. Mrs. Moore did not attend the hearings; she felt that the NEA was prejudiced in favor of the teachers.

After reviewing all the testimony, the panel published its findings. The NEA report identified several issues in the conflict. Two of these issues were: What are the rights of parents and community members in textbook selection? And what are the responsibilities of educators? The report concluded that parents and community members have a right to serve as advisors or consultants. But educators have the responsibility to act as decision makers.

The report also identified several causes of the conflict. Kanawha County was a community divided by differences in incomes, life-styles, religoius beliefs, and educational values. The differences between well-paid city dwellers and poor rural families were particularly noticeable. Liberal school administrators had failed to communicate effectively with conservative farmers and miners. The school board had failed to respond swiftly to the first textbook protests. And the crisis was made worse by "right-wing extremist groups." These groups included the John Birch Society, Citizens for Decency Through Law, the Heritage Foundation, the National Parents League, and the Ku Klux Klan.

The report commented on the seven guidelines for textbook selection: "If the recently adopted guidelines were interpreted in the way that the [antitext group] appears to have interpreted them, . . . [they] would impose upon the public schools the task of indoctrinating students to one system of cultural and religious values, inflexible and unexamined." For example, the NEA panel members feared that the guidelines would prevent students from learning about a variety of topics in American history—Watergate, because the complete record contained swearing; the black and Indian experiences, because those stories might promote racial hatred; or even the Kanawha County textbook conflict, because some citizens used violence instead of legal procedures.

The report also criticized the new methods for textbook selection. The panel members felt that the new rules would turn parents into censors. And, possibly, the antitext protestors would be able to impose their ideas about education on the whole county.

Finally, the NEA report offered some recommendations for future action. School administrators should try to improve communications with area residents. The school board should hold its meetings in various parts of the county. Alternative schools that focused on basic learning skills might even be considered.

On January 30, 1975, the United States District Court for the Southern District of West Virginia decided a minor case that grew out of the Kanawha County war. Gary Williams, Sr., was a parent of school age children in the county. He claimed that his First, Ninth, and Fourteenth Amendment rights had been violated by the board's decision to use the controversial textbooks. The U.S. Supreme Court has said that the Ninth Amendment includes the right of privacy.

The main issue before the district court was whether the books created an antireligious atmosphere in the classroom. Williams's attorney argued that the texts offended his client's religious beliefs. So the parent had to remove his children from the public school and place them in a private school. Williams was still paying taxes to support the public school system. Therefore, the board should pay the extra costs for his children's private schooling.

But in the case of *Williams* v. *The Board of Education of the County of Kanawha,* Judge K. K. Hall dismissed the parent's complain. Judge Hall understood that the books offended Williams, but he ruled that the use of the texts did not prevent the family from practicing its religion. He noted that "the First Amendment . . . does not guarantee that nothing . . . offensive to any religion will be taught in the schools." He quoted from *Epperson* v. *Arkansas* in explaining the relationship between government and religion: "Government in our democracy, state and national, must be neutral in matters of religious theory, doctrine, and practice. It may not be hostile to any religion or to the advocacy of no-religion." The judge advised Williams to take his complaint directly to the board or to vote against board members when they came up for reelection.

In other court cases the people accused of various violent crimes were tried, convicted, and fined or imprisoned. The charges against the three board members and the superintendent of schools were quietly dropped.

What sense can we make of this complicated affair? The Kanawha County war was different from the Presidents Council battle. For example, several hundred books came under fire, not just one. Dozens of topics, not just life in Spanish Harlem, were endangered by censorship. Many citizens' groups, not just a handful, fought for their own points of view.

Alice Moore, the Gablers, the fundamentalist ministers, the Christian-American Parents, the Concerned Citizens of Kanawha County, and the striking miners were all pressure groups for the need to protect. These people wanted to safeguard students from what they considered dangerous ideas about sex, race, religion, privacy, and patriotism. The language arts teachers' committee, the school administrators, the non-fundamentalist ministers, and the Authors League of America fought for the right to know. These people wanted to open students' minds to ways of life and thought different from those in Kanawha County.

The school board was caught in the middle. It tried to work out a compromise. In the end the board members accepted the textbooks. But they also established guidelines and methods that made future choices more difficult. The National Education Association tried to be fair and made suggestions to both sides. The district court ruled against a protesting parent. But the judge also stressed the importance of government neutrality in religious matters. All things considered, the war over the textbooks was probably a draw.

The Kanawha County Coalition for Quality Education, a pro-textbook group, may have come closest to identifying the conflict's real cause. According to *The New Republic* magazine, the coalition felt that "Watergate, a changing set of values, Vietnam, inflation, and a host of other confusing trends in the social order . . . brought about a situation in which people [were] frustrated, confused, angry and fearful. When such a condition exists," the organization explained, "there is a desire on the part of human beings to seek simple solutions to complicated problems, react to change with hostility, and meet authority . . . with . . . lack of trust. . . . The textbooks [became] a convenient scapegoat."

Minority groups, including fundamentalists, want to make sure that their views are accurately described in textbooks. They also want to have a say in textbook selection. But should they be able to ban so many books that students get only one view of the world? Do children need this much protection? Isn't minority censorship just as threatening to a democracy as majority censorship?

The next chapter shows that involving citizens' groups in the textbook selection process does not always prevent school book battles.

Trouble in Strongsville

Susan Lee Minarcini was a high school student in Strongsville, Ohio, a suburb of Cleveland. Susan's parents, along with the parents of four other students, filed a lawsuit against the Strongsville City School District.

The suit charged that the five-member board of education had violated students' First and Fourteenth Amendment rights. Specifically, the board had deprived students of their rights to academic freedom, due process, and equal protection of the laws. Board members had allegedly violated these constitutional rights by refusing to accept teachers' choices of three novels. The books were *Catch-22* by Joseph Heller and *God Bless You, Mr. Rosewater* and *Cat's Cradle* by Kurt Vonnegut, Jr. The American Civil Liberties Union helped the students and their parents with the suit.

The trouble began in the spring of 1972. The English Department of a high school in the district recommended the purchase of several books for the following fall. On April 4 the sixteen-member Citizens' Textbook Committee accepted all of the department's recommendations except for *Catch-22*. A majority of the committee members objected to the use of the book as a required text. The committee did, however, accept *God Bless You, Mr. Rosewater* as a substitute for the Heller novel.

Catch-22 was published in 1961 and it has been described as a "comic novel about World War II." The book's main character is Captain John Yossarian. He is a bombadier with the 256th U.S. Air Force Squadron stationed on a small island in the Mediterranean. After seeing a number of his friends killed in action, Captain Yossarian tries to get out of combat duty by acting insane. But the catch in his plan is military regulation number 22. This rule says that anyone who tries to get out of combat duty must be considered sane. No sane person would go into combat willingly. So the novel is really about the craziness of war.

Generally, critics gave *Catch-22* high marks. Nelson Algren, a famous writer, said: "This novel is not merely the best American novel to come out of World War II; it is the best American novel that has come out of anywhere in years." Paramount Pictures released a movie version of the book in 1970. And by mid-1971 more than seven million copies of the novel had been sold. A book reviewer for *The San Francisco Chronicle*, William Hogan, gave one reason for the novel's popularity: "The youngsters seem to find in Heller a voice, a rallying point, a rationale and a fresh breeze of protest against the more zany military establishment."

Not all the reviewers were impressed, though. Some criticized the book's graphic descriptions of sex and violence. Whitney Balliett, a reviewer for *The New Yorker*, complained that Heller's novel was filled with "sour jokes, stage anger, [and] dirty words."

God Bless You, Mr. Rosewater, published in 1965, received

less attention than *Catch-22*. Among other things, Vonnegut's novel dealt with the problems of loving unlovable people and the American drive for wealth. Melvin Maddocks, a reviewer for *The Christian Science Monitor*, called it "one of the best of the 'black humor' school." Black humor is comedy that deals with serious subjects such as death.

The Strongsville Board of Education took most of the Citizens' Textbook Committee's advice. The entire board approved all of the English Department's recommendations except for *Catch-22*. A decision on the Vonnegut novel as a substitute selection was put off for a later date. On May 18, 1972, several English teachers tried to persuade board members to reconsider their rejection of Heller's novel. *God Bless You, Mr. Rosewater* was also discussed at this meeting.

On June 8 the school board again voted not to buy *Catch-22*. At a special meeting nine days later, the board members refused to talk about the English Department's second choice—*God Bless You, Mr. Rosewater*—even though it had been accepted by the citizens' committee.

At another special meeting on August 19, the board members also refused to consider the English Department's third choice, *Cat's Cradle*, which was published in 1963. This Vonnegut novel is "an offbeat science-versus-religion story." It focuses on two main characters—a physicist and a prophet. The physicist invents "ice-nine," a substance that freezes all the water in the world. The prophet preaches a gospel of doom and silly sayings. Graham Greene, a famous British novelist, called *Cat's Cradle* "one of the three best novels of the year by one of the most able living writers." The book had been used in Strongsville schools in 1969.

But in 1972 the board of education decided that *Cat's Cradle*, *God Bless You, Mr. Rosewater*, and *Catch-22* were "adult-oriented and, therefore, less suitable for use as curriculum text for grades ten through twelve than other available novels." On September 14 the board finally approved the English Department's fourth choice—*Travels with Charlie* by John Steinbeck. Unlike the other three novels, *Travels with Charlie* is not an example of black humor.

Five families, including the Minarcinis, went to court. They were apparently motivated by a 1969 Supreme Court ruling that recognized students' rights: "School officials do not possess absolute authority over their students. Students in school as well as out of school are 'persons' under the Constitution. They are possessed of fundamental rights which the State must respect."

The families argued that the school board had unconstitutionally censored classroom material. The board members had failed to consult experts to determine whether the books would harm students in any way. Therefore, the board had rejected the three novels without following proper procedure and without giving good reasons.

The United States District Court for the Northern District of Ohio decided *Minarcini* v. *Strongsville City School District* on August 9, 1974. Judge Robert B. Krupansky wrote the opinion. He identified three questions in the case. Did the board have the authority to select textbooks for the district? Did the board make its selections in a proper way? Were constitutional issues at stake? Judge Krupansky answered yes to the first two questions, and no to the third.

The judge explained his answers. Ohio law gave the board the authority to select textbooks, and the board had followed proper procedure in making its selections. All meetings had been open to the public, and the board members had consulted enough teachers, administrators, and citizens to make reasonable decisions. Also, the members were educated and experienced enough themselves to make sound judgments. Finally, the board did not violate anyone's

First Amendment rights because it did not forbid teachers, students, or librarians to read or discuss the three novels *outside* of class.

Judge Krupansky based his conclusions on various court precedents. He quoted from *Presidents Council, District 25 v. Community School Board No. 25:* "Censorship . . . is an inescapable aspect of operating a school system." In other words, *someone* has to decide what students will be allowed to read and what they will not be allowed to read. The judge also referred to *Epperson v. Arkansas.* He noted that courts should not interfere with school board procedures unless constitutional issues are clearly at stake.

But these were not the last words on the matter. The five families took their case to the next highest court. Interestingly, the United States Court of Appeals for the Sixth Circuit discussed facts that Judge Krupansky had not mentioned in his opinion.

Appellate Court Judge George C. Edwards Jr., said that the Strongsville board had passed two resolutions ordering the removal of *Catch-22* and *Cat's Cradle* from school libraries. The resolutions were meant to discourage students from reading the novels outside of class. Presumably, Judge Krupansky had not mentiond these facts because he had dismissed the families' complaint concerning the libraries.

Judge Edwards also identified the three questions in the case differently than the lower court judge had. Did the board have the authority to approve or purchase textbooks for the district? Did the board have the authority to remove books from the school library? Did the board infringe on teachers' academic freedom? The appellate court judge answered yes to the first question, and no to the second and third.

Judge Edwards agreed that Ohio law gave the board the authority to approve or purchase textbooks. But the board did not have the authority to remove books from the school library. On this issue Edwards felt that Krupansky had misinterpreted the *Presidents Council* precedent. Edwards explained that libraries were different from classrooms: "A library is a storehouse of knowledge. When created for a public school it is an important privilege created by the state for the benefit of the students in the school. That privilege is not subject to being withdrawn by succeeding school boards whose members might desire to 'winnow' the library for books the content of which occasioned their displeasure or disapproval."

According to Judge Edwards the only reason the Heller and Vonnegut novels were removed from the library was that one board member didn't like black humor. The school board's records for July 17, 1972, showed that Dr. Arthur L. Crain had made the following report: "It is recommended that *God Bless You, Mr. Rosewater* not be purchased, either as a textbook, supplemental reading book or library book. The book is completely sick. One secretary read it for one-half hour and handed it back to the reviewer with the written comment, 'GARBAGE.' . . . It is also recommended that *Cat's Cradle*, which was written by the same character (Vennegutter) . . . be withdrawn immediately and all copies disposed of." In reversing the lower court's decision on the school library issue, Judge Edwards recognized the students' right to know: "Here we are concerned with the right of students to receive information which they and their teachers desire them to have. First Amendment protection of the right to know has frequently been recognized in the past. . . . We believe that . . . recent cases . . . serve to establish firmly both the First Amendment right to know . . . and the [right] of the student plaintiffs to raise the issue."

On the third question, however, Judge Edwards agreed that the teachers' academic freedom had not been violated. He admitted that the two book-removal resolutions probably did have a "chilling effect" on classroom discussions. But the evidence did not clearly show that the board ever forbade teachers to talk about the novels in school. On August 30, 1976, the judge declared the resolutions "null and void." He also ordered the board to replace the books on the library shelves. The school district appealed to the United States Surpeme Court. But the high court refused to review the case.

The Strongsville trouble was more like the Presidents Council battle than the Kanawha County war. It was a relatively simple affair. The value of only three books was questioned. What those books had in common was a particular view of life. And only a small group of citizens became involved in the conflict.

The five students and their parents, the high school English Department, and the American Civil Liberties Union supported the right to know. They wanted students to understand a significant type of American literature. The school board was concerned about the need to protect. Most of the members wanted to keep students from being exposed to a point of view that they considered "sick." The Citizens' Textbook Committee offered a compromise. It rejected the more extreme example of black humor *(Catch-22)* but accepted a milder example *(God Bless You, Mr. Rosewater)*.

Although the district court sided with the school board, that court did not have the final say. The appellate court upheld the board's authority to select textbooks. But unlike the Second Circuit Court in the *Presidents Council* case, the Sixth Circuit Court denied the board's authority to remove already purchased library books. So the *Minarcini* case was mainly a win for the defenders of the right to know.

Despite its relative simplicity, the trouble in Strongsville was an important matter. *Minarcini* was the first school censorship case to support the *student's* right to know. The appellate court viewed the school library as a "marketplace of ideas." There students could discover books beyond the classroom. Finally, the *Minarcini* decision indicated that a school board's personal tastes could not be allowed to overrule a department's recommendations and a citizens' committee's judgment.

The *Presidents Council* case served as a precedent for the *Minarcini* ruling. *Minarcini*, in turn, became a precedent for later school book battles. The next chapter shows how the meaning of these two decisions became clearer in the settlement of later cases.

Chapter 4

"The City to a Young Girl"

I think it can be said without contradiction that I am certainly no prude in certain matters—but the complaint of a father made to me yesterday about passages in a book his daughter obtained at the high school library has almost made me sick to my stomach to think that such a book could be obtained in any school—let alone one here in Chelsea.

I want to bring this matter to the attention of our Administrators and I want to make certain that no such filth will be distributed in our schools.

Quite frankly, more than that, I want a complete review of how it was possible for such garbage to even get on bookshelves where 14 year old high school—ninth graders—could obtain them.

Those words were part of an article that appeared on May 19, 1977, in a community newspaper called *The Chelsea Record*. They were written by Andrew P. Quigley, the paper's owner and publisher. He was also the chairman of the Chelsea School Committee. The committee was a seven-member group elected to operate the Chelsea public schools. Chelsea is a small town in Massachusetts just northeast of Boston.

The book that Quigley was upset about was an anthology called *Male and Female Under 18*, a collection of prose and poetry written by elementary and high school students. The passage that Quigley objected to was a poem entitled "The City to a Young Girl." It had been written by a fifteen-year-old Brooklyn, New York student. In the poem she had complained about sex-starved men who saw her only as "a good piece of meat." "City" contained several sexual slang words that most parents would not expect their children to learn in school.

Before Quigley wrote his article, Sonja Coleman—the Chelsea High School librarian—had ordered a collection of one thousand reading books. Any of the books that were judged unsuitable for Chelsea students could be exchanged. When the collection was delivered, Coleman looked at all of the books, but she did not have time to read every page.

One of the books was *Male and Female Under 18*. The librarian knew that the anthology's publisher had a good reputation for literature for young adults. She also recognized the names of the collection's two editors. They were highly respected professionals.

The librarian read the book's introduction and skimmed its table of contents. But she did not read "The City to a Young Girl." Coleman thought that *Male and Female* would help students taking an English Department course called Adolescent Literature. So in March 1976, she placed a copy of the anthology in the Chelsea High School library.

Almost a year later Chairman Quigley received a telephone call from an irate parent. The parent was angry about a book that his daughter had borrowed from the school library. The book was *Male and Female Under 18.* The father felt that the poem "City" contained offensive language.

Quigley went to the parent's home, got the book, and read the poem. He decided that it was "filthy." He did not read any other part of the collection nor did he talk with any other adults about the anthology. Nevertheless, he concluded that the book should be removed from the library.

On the same evening that Quigley picked up the book, he scheduled an emergency meeting of the Chelsea School Committee. The purpose of the meeting was to consider the "objectionable, salacious and obscene material being made available in books in the High School library." Then he wrote the article that appeared in his newspaper.

Before the meeting was held, Quigley gave copies of the poem to the three other male committee members. He did not give copies to any of the three female members because he thought that they would be offended by the poem's language. He also thought that at least two of the women would agree to an investigation of library book selection procedures without even reading "City."

At the May 23, 1977, emergency meeting, Quigley repeated his concerns about *Male and Female.* One of the other male committee members said: "The book is lewd and leaves nothing to the imagination. It's outright obnoxious." Chairman Quigley then asked Superintendent of Schools Vincent McGee to find out how the anthology was selected for the library. McGee warned the chairman that the committee was "setting in motion a chain of events that might lead to censorship."

Three days later the superintendent submitted a report on the book. He concluded: "The text reflects the goals the editors were attempting to accomplish. I believe the book is sound and has educational value with the exception of the passage objected to and one other word in one other poem." However, McGee agreed to remove *Male and Female* from the library temporarily; that is, until a final decision was made to remove the whole book or only the "City" pages.

The principal of Chelsea High School explained the library book selection process. And Quigley ended this meeting by asking McGee to determine if librarian Coleman had knowingly ordered "trash." The chairman said that the committee would then decide whether she was "the type of person we want to continue in that position."

On June 14 Quigley published a statement by Coleman. The librarian asserted that the poem "City" was not obscene. She also maintained that the book *Male and Female* should not have been removed from the school library without the type of hearing recommended by the American Library Association. Quigley replied that he was "shocked and extremely disappointed" by the librarian's attitude.

About six weeks later the Chelsea School Committee voted to ban the entire book. A motion to make the anthology available to students with parental permission was defeated. The committee members also discussed transferring Coleman out of the library and into a classroom for her "mistake" in ordering *Male and Female.*

Several students, their parents, librarian Coleman, the chairwoman of the English Department, and an English teacher formed the Right to Read Defense Committee of Chelsea. On August 3 this group sued the Chelsea School Committee and the superintendent. The suit charged the committee with violating the First Amendment rights of Chelsea High School students, teachers, and librarians.

Quigley reacted to the lawsuit in *The Chelsea Record:* "Who needs employees that will fight to keep the kind of tasteless, filthy trash that is contained in the poem we voted to remove? I may even call a special meeting to discuss what we'll do with these insubordinate teachers." He also circulated petitions to show that most Chelsea citizens disapproved of the poem. Then the Chelsea School Committee sent copies of "City" to thirty clergymen for their opinions. Two supported the ban.

On August 17 the school committee's lawyer recommended that the committee members adopt two resolutions to explain their position. The first resolution said that the committee had banned *Male and Female* because it dealt with sex education in an unhealthy way. The second promised that the committee would not punish the librarian, teachers, or students for filing their lawsuit.

Two days later the United States District Court for Massachusetts issued a temporary restraining order. Until the case was finally decided, the Chelsea School Committee could not penalize anyone involved in the suit. Additionally, the book had to be returned to the library and made available to students with parental permission to read it.

On August 29 Quigley ran an editorial in his newspaper. Among other things, the article said that the lawsuit "must not and cannot be allowed to intimidate the Committee from doing what has to be done to root out all the "filthy" literature that is being circulated in the High School under the guise of education."

In the spring of 1978, District Court Judge Joseph L. Tauro heard arguments on both sides. The Right to Read Defense Committee claimed that the Chelsea School Committee had acted unconstitutionally in banning *Male and Female.* The school committee argued that it had the authority to oversee the Chelsea High School curriculum. The school committee also claimed that it had an *unlimited* authority to remove books from the school library.

On July 5, 1978, Judge Tauro decided the case of *Right to Read Defense Committee of Chelsea* v. *School Committee of the City of Chelsea* in favor of the Right to Read group. He said that the issue was whether a school committee has the same authority to remove a book from a school library that it does to select a book. He concluded that such a committee has an unlimited right to select books. But its right to remove books is limited by the First Amendment.

In explaining his decision, the judge said that "a school should be a readily accessible warehouse of ideas." He also observed that the First Amendment was not like a coat that students and teachers had to take off when they entered the classroom.

Judge Tauro then discussed the *Presidents Council* case. The Chelsea School Committee assumed that this precedent gave school committees everywhere the unlimited authority to remove books from school libraries for any reason. This assumption was incorrect. Actually, the Second Circuit Court in the *Presidents Council* case had set clearly defined limits on a committee's authority. Books could be removed *only* if they were considered obsolete, irrelevant, or improperly selected in the first place.

There was no evidence in the *Right to Read* case that *Male and Female Under 18* was out-of-date, unimportant to students, or chosen without following proper procedures. In presenting its arguments, the school committee had not even tried to prove that the anthology was obscene. Judge Tauro concluded that *Male and Female* was banned solely because the school committee members considered "the theme and language of 'City' to be offensive."

The judge cited a 1977 Supreme Court ruling which said that "the reasons underlying the actions of school officials may determine their constitutionality." He criticized the Chelsea School Committee for passing its August 17 resolution saying that the book was not good sex education. Judge Tauro felt that this action was simply an attempt to hide the committee's real reasons for removing the book. In fact, he decided that the "sex education" resolution was merely a *pretext*, a false reason meant to hide a real one.

Next Judge Tauro quoted from the *Minarcini* case: "Neither the State of Ohio nor the Strongsville School Board was under any federal constitutional compulsion to provide a library for the Strongsville High School. . . . Once having created such a privilege for the benefit of its students, however, neither body could place conditions on the use of the library which were related solely to the social or political tastes of school board members." So once the Chelsea School Committee purchased *Male and Female* for its library, the committee members could not remove the book because of their own personal tastes.

The judge admitted that "City" was not "a polite poem." Its "tough" language might offend some people. However, the poem was not obscene. And it was "challenging" and "thought-provoking."

Most of all Judge Tauro was concerned about the precedent he might set if he allowed the school committee to ban the book or censor the poem. "If this work may be removed by a committee hostile to its language or theme, then the precedent is set for removal of any other work. The prospect of successive school committees 'sanitizing' the school library of views [different] from their own is alarming, whether they do it book by book or one page at a time. What is at stake here is the right to read and be exposed to controversial thoughts and language—a valuable right subject to First Amendment protection."

Finally, the judge observed: "The most effective antidote to the poison of mindless orthodoxy is ready access to a broad sweep of ideas and philosophies. There is no danger in such exposure. The danger is in mind control."

The *Right to Read* case resembled *Minarcini* more than *Presidents Council*. Mr. Quigley, like Dr. Crain, persuaded the school board to remove a book from the school library because of his own personal tastes. Judge Tauro, like Judge Edwards, refused to allow this removal because of the First Amendment. Also, Tauro agreed with Edwards's view of the school library as a "marketplace of ideas."

Like *Minarcini*, the *Right to Read* decision was a victory for the right to know. The defense committee members wanted students to see how the city appeared to a young girl even though her language was coarse and crude. The school committee members wanted to protect students from exposure to "dirty" words in school.

Because of its resemblance to *Minarcini*, the *Right to Read* decision broke no new ground. Its importance lay in that it clarified the meaning of the *Presidents Council* and *Minarcini* rulings. Those two cases seemed to reach opposite conclusions. The Second Circuit Court said that a school board had the authority to remove a book from a school library. The Sixth Circuit Court said that it did not have that authority.

In the *Right to Read* case, the Massachusetts District Court said that a school board's authority to *select* books was absolute, total, and unquestionable. However, a board's authority to *remove* books depended on its reasons for doing so. Although it was all right for board members to remove old books because the school library needed room for new ones, it was not all right to remove books because board members suddenly disapproved of them. In fact, removal of school library books for personal, social, or political reasons amounted to unconstitutional censorship.

We have seen that objection to a book's sexual language has been the reason for the attempted removal of some school library books. The next chapter shows that disapproval of a textbook's *racial* viewpoint can also lead to attempted censorship.

Chapter 5

Mississippi: Conflict and Change

The state of Mississippi has been the scene of much racial conflict and change over the years. In 1962 James Meredith enrolled as the first black student at the University of Mississippi. Riots broke out and two people died. The next year Medgar Evers, a field secretary for the National Association for the Advancement of Colored People, was shot and killed. In 1964 three voter registration workers were murdered near Philadelphia, Mississippi. Five years later Charles Evers, the brother of Medgar, became the mayor of Fayette. He was the first black mayor in the state since the end of the Civil War. Some Mississippians wanted their children to learn about the historical reasons for these conflicts and changes. Others did not.

In the fall of 1974, the State Textbook Purchasing Board told educational publishers that it wanted to buy books for a ninth-grade course called Mississippi History. The Steck-Vaughn Company submitted a book entitled *Your Mississippi* by Dr. John K. Bettersworth. Pantheon Books submitted *Mississippi: Conflict and Change* by Dr. James W. Loewen and Dr. Charles Sallis.

Both texts had to be reviewed by a seven-member rating committee. The governor appointed four of the members, and the state superintendent of education appointed three. The committee that evaluated the Mississippi history books included five whites and two blacks.

On August 28 the rating committee members attended a meeting sponsored by the Purchasing Board. At this meeting they received information on how to review textbooks. The information consisted of publications called "Mississippi Textbook Adoption" and "Suggested Criteria for Textbook Selection." Among other things, the "Suggested Criteria" said that each book proposed for adoption should have a teacher's edition. The information also included evaluation forms and a list of certified publishers' representatives.

Between August 28 and October 23, representatives visited the committee members. The Steck-Vaughn representative gave each member an advance copy of the teacher's edition that would accompany *Your Mississippi*. The Pantheon representative did not have a teacher's edition for *Conflict and Change*. At the trial that occurred later, there was conflicting testimony about what the Pantheon representative told the committee members. Some said he told them that no teacher's edition would be available, and others testified that he said one would be available at a later date.

On October 23 the rating committee turned in its evaluation forms. All five of the white committee members gave *Conflict and Change* "no rating." This meant that the State Textbook Purchasing Board could not let schools consider the book for the Mississippi history course. Consequently, the Board adopted *Your Mississippi* for at least four years.

State law required the committee members to explain their reasons for rejecting a text on their evaluation forms. John Turnipseed simply called *Conflict and Change* "unsuitable for classroom use." Howard Riales identified a picture and a paragraph in the book as "objectionable." He went on to say: "This is only two examples of many in the book. Continuous coverage of isolated incidents of the mis-treatment of slaves and blacks by whites could easily lead the readers to believe that all slaves and blacks were treated in the same manner. I feel that this book is too racially oriented and does not concentrate sufficiently on the areas as suggested in the criteria." Virginia McElhaney commented: "I do not feel that the ideas concentrated on this text are expressed in terms of the junior high school student. Perhaps for college level and mature adult. It does not meet requirement as a textbook. Readability level too high. I do not feel that the overall content presents a true picture of the history of Mississippi in terms of the prescribed course prerequisite."

Loewen and Sallis, the two authors of *Mississippi: Conflict and Change*, sued the rating committee, the Purchasing Board, the governor, the state superintendent, and other state officials. They were joined in their suit by students, teachers, ministers, and civil rights leaders. The authors claimed that the rejection of their book deprived them of their First, Thirteenth, and Fourteenth Amendment rights. The Thirteenth Amendment abolished slavery.

The plaintiffs (the people bringing the suit) asked the court to order the defendants (the people being sued) to do several things:

- To put *Conflict and Change* on the list of state-approved texts that schools could order
- To stop discriminating against books that presented nontraditional views of Mississippi history

- To use fairer procedures in selecting future textbooks
- To consider new texts more often

The case of *Loewen* v. *Turnipseed* was tried in eight days. At the trial the rating committee members gave reasons for rejecting *Conflict and Change* other than the ones they had written on their evaluation forms. They feared that the book would stir up racial tensions in classrooms. The Pantheon representative had failed to provide them with teacher's editions. The defendants' lawyer also argued that a decision for the plaintiffs would constitute federal interference with the state's right to choose what books students may read.

U.S. District Court Judge Orma R. Smith of the Northern District of Mississippi decided the case on April 2, 1980. He ruled in favor of the plaintiffs. And he concluded that the defendants had deprived the authors of their First Amendment rights to freedom of speech and press as well as their Fourteenth Amendment right to due process.

Like Judge Tauro in the *Right to Read* case, Judge Smith felt that the committee members' stated reasons for rejecting *Conflict and Change* were not their real reasons. He noted that the "Suggested Criteria for Textbook Selection" did not require the submission of a teacher's edition *along with* the book. The criteria merely said that a teacher's edition had to be available if the text were adopted.

The judge also noted that the textbook already contained many suggestions for class discussions, special projects, and field trips. And he quoted from an educational magazine article on the book: " 'By any reasonable criteria, including those used by the Mississippi review committee, *Conflict and Change* is not only eligible for adoption, but is far superior in format and content to all history textbooks we have seen.' "

On the due process issue, Judge Smith decided that the state had clearly set up procedures to prevent publishers from challenging a book's rejection. The Textbook Chapter of the Mississippi Code had been passed in 1960. Records of the debate over the code showed the state legislature's motives. It wanted "to eliminate allegedly controversial material from the schools' curriculum, and to insure that only the views of those in authority would be communicated to school children."

During the legislative debate, Governor Ross Barnett had said: "Failure of the House to act favorably upon this bill will, I very much fear, hamper our efforts to clean up our public school textbooks and give our children the instruction material they must have if they are to be properly informed of the Southern and true American way of life."

Other evidence presented at the trial indicated that the legislature passed the code to give the governor and the state superintendent of education unusual power. The code gave these two officials "the power to control the destiny of any textbook offered for adoption by the State Purchasing Board." So Judge Smith concluded that the rating committee's real reasons for rejecting *Conflict and Change* were racial. That is, the committee members wanted to prevent Mississippi school children from learning about integration and "to perpetuate ideas of segregation and discrimination."

The main issue in *Loewen v. Turnipseed*, however, was whether state officials have an *unlimited* authority to decide what books children may read in school. Again like Judge Tauro, Judge Smith refused to grant a governing body such sweeping power. He commented: "There must be some method by which [unlimited] governmental control over 'the free exchange' of ideas can be checked." Otherwise, reasonable governmental regulation becomes unreasonable.

The judge then went on to discuss broader issues. "The field of education," he said, "is one which needs particular constitutional protection. This is so because educational issues such as academic freedom are fundamentally linked with First Amendment guarantees." He admitted that the First Amendment does not specifically mention freedom to teach, but he quoted from another court opinion to make his point: " 'The First Amendment references to freedom of speech and of the press are designed to assure the free exchange in the general marketplace of ideas. Academic freedom, it can be argued, is the adaptation of those specific constitutional rights to protect communication in the classroom as a special marketplace of ideas.' "

He reminded the defendants that, according to *Epperson v. Arkansas,* courts should not interfere with states' rights in educational matters *unless constitutional issues are at stake.* Judge Smith proceeded to explain that *Loewen v. Turnipseed* "is a case which 'directly and sharply' implicates constitutional values. It does so because the defendants have provided no method by which the plaintiffs may safeguard their First Amendment freedoms."

So the judge decided to provide a method. He ordered the defendants to put *Mississippi: Conflict and Change* on the list of state-approved texts that schools could purchase. But he refused to recommend the Loewen and Sallis book over the Bettersworth book. "The court cannot now place the judicial seal of approval on the ideas found in one book, and [belittle] the ideas found in another. To do so would violate the same constitutional principles [of free speech] which the court now seeks to protect."

Neither would Judge Smith change the state's procedures for selecting textbooks. "The court should not undertake to dictate to the defendants a plan of textbook approval. Underlying notions of federalism do not allow the court to supervise state administrative proceedings."

The *Loewen* case resembled the *Right to Read* case in two ways. First, the Mississippi District Court considered the rating committee's expressed reasons for rejecting *Conflict and Change* to be mere pretexts for their real racial reasons. Second, the court ruled that a state's authority to make decisions on children's school books was *limited* by the First Amendment and by the state's reasons for its decisions.

Like Judge Tauro in *Right to Read* and Justice Fortas in *Epperson*, Judge Smith feared the spread of *orthodoxy* into the classroom. Orthodoxy is the presentation of one official view of the truth to the exclusion of all other views. And like Tauro in the Chelsea matter and Edwards in *Minarcini*, Smith also saw the school as a marketplace or warehouse of ideas where different points of view could be studied and discussed.

Loewen v. *Turnipseed* was yet another win for the right to know. The plaintiffs in this case wanted students to learn about the history of slavery, segregation, and discrimination that led to racial conflict and change in Mississippi. The defendants wanted to protect students from upsetting ideas that might open old wounds and start new troubles. The district court sided more with the plaintiffs than with the defendants. However, it did take a traditional states'-rights position on Mississippi's procedures for selecting textbooks.

Loewen was not a landmark case, one that signals a dramatic turning point. But it was important because it indicated that the federal courts would let neither governors nor state legislatures engage in the practice of turning history into propaganda. In other words, officials responsible for a state's curriculum could not purposely try to make the past seem better or worse than it actually was.

The next chapter shows that different courts have taken different views of academic freedom, especially in regard to high school students.

Chapter 6

Book Burning in Indiana

The books made a fine bonfire one cold winter day in a small Midwestern town.

On December 15, 1977, the Senior Citizens Club of Warsaw, Indiana, carried forty copies of *Values Clarification* to a parking lot. There they doused the books with gasoline and set them on fire. One local school board member said that now teachers would "have no problem knowing the will of this community."

The community he referred to was located in the northern part of Indiana, about halfway between South Bend and Fort Wayne. Most of Warsaw's middle-class residents worked in small local industries. In 1977 the town's population stood at about 9,600.

The book-burning incident began during the summer day of July 19. On that date the Warsaw School Board ordered *Values Clarification* to be "thrown out, removed, banned, destroyed, and forbidden."

The text had been used in a Warsaw High School elective course for two years. It contained exercises in which students were asked how they felt about controversial topics like divorce, marijuana, and premarital sex. Apparently, some parents thought that these questions were too personal. Others presumably feared that the book promoted a philosophy of ethical relativism. This philosophy says that there are no absolute, cut and dried standards of right and wrong. It holds that the rightness and wrongness of human actions depend on time, place, and circumstance.

On August 25 the school board also ordered the discontinuation of several elective high school courses. These courses were Black Literature, Gothic Literature, Science Fiction, Folklore and Legends, and Whatever Happened to Mankind?

Teresa Burnau was scheduled to teach an English course entitled Women in Literature. But before classes started in September, the principal of Warsaw High School summoned the teacher to his office. He forbade her to use two books that she had ordered for the course. The books were an anthology called *Growing Up Female in America* and a novel called *The Stepford Wives.* The principal's reason for banning the books was that "someone in the community might be offended by their criticism of traditional roles for women."

Growing Up Female in America "presents glimpses into the lives of American women of different ethnic, religious, and social groups." Most critics gave the anthology positive reviews. Deborah Halprin of the *Library Journal* said that it put "the women's movement of today into historical perspective." And B. B. Watson of *The Nation* magazine called it "a refreshing change from the . . . claims and counterclaims [of books on feminism]."

The Stepford Wives is about suburban housewives who are murdered by their chauvinistic husbands. Submissive, obedient robots replace the women. The novel received mixed comments. In

Saturday Review Webster Schott noted that the author Ira Levin "has . . . the magician's touch; he casts a spell, and [the book] becomes believable." On the other hand, the critic for *The Christian Science Monitor* remarked: "It's bound to be read however poor its quality. . . . Mr. Levin isn't merely anti-woman. He's anti-people."

In mid-October the principal forbade Burnau to use another work—*Go Ask Alice*. This book is a diary by an unidentified teenage girl who died of a drug overdose shortly after her sixteenth birthday. The principal's reason for banning the book was that it contained "dirty" words.

The reviewer for *The Christian Science Monitor* was well aware of objections to the diary but was also quite definite about its value: "Many parents will not want their children to read [this book]. . . . The subject is unpleasant, the language sometimes crude, the experiences often horrifying. And yet—precisely because of this reluctance to expose one's children to such material—the book must be read. More than anything else, it was the lack of communication that 'Alice' felt between herself and the world of her parents, teachers, and friends, and her lack of knowledge about drugs, that proved fatal." The *Library Journal* strongly recommended the work too.

After the banning of *Go Ask Alice*, the principal sent a directive to the faculty. The order said that teachers should turn in all materials which "might be objectionable." An English teacher brought copies of *Student Critic* to the principal's office. The text included two four-letter words. The pages containing the words were cut out before the books were returned to classrooms.

Around Thanksgiving Burnau was told that she could no longer teach *The Bell Jar* by Sylvia Plath—even though Burnau suggested using parental permission slips. Plath's book is an autobiographical novel about a nineteen-year-old girl's struggle with mental illness. The author committed suicide a month before the book was published.

Phoebe Adams of *The Atlantic Monthly* wrote: "It is not really a good novel, although extremely promising as first novels go." Robert Scholes of *The New York Times Book Review* called Plath's work "clear and readable . . . witty and disturbing." He went on to say that "this is not a potboiler . . . it is literature."

To show support for the principal's actions, The Warsaw Senior Citizens Club burned the copies of *Values Clarification* ten days before Christmas.

On April 17, 1978, the school board notified several teachers that their contracts would not be renewed. Among the fired employees were Teresa Burnau and Joann Dupont. Dupont was the secretary of the Warsaw Teachers' Union and a frequent critic of board policies. The board members did not say how the two women had failed to meet their responsibilities; they simply accused them of "displaying poor attitudes."

A local politician suspected a conspiracy between the board and the publisher of the town's only newspaper. The publisher had played an important part in appointing four of the newest board members. In a newspaper advertisement the politician commented: "The current thinly disguised union-busting activities promoted by the local media monopoly have ruined the careers of several very capable teachers while forcing others out of the community."

In May a student newspaper objected to the teacher firings. The paper was promptly discontinued as an extracurricular activity.

During the spring of 1979, Brooke Zykan, a seventeen-year-old Warsaw High School student, sued the school district. Her brother Blair, who was a former student, and their parents were also listed as plaintiffs. The attorney for the Zykans was Joseph P. Bauer, an American Civil Liberties Union lawyer and a law professor at the University of Notre Dame.

The Zykan suit claimed that the district had violated students' First and Fourteenth Amendment rights. Attorney Bauer said that the issue in the case was "whether a school board has a right to remove books and courses and fire teachers because they [conflict] with the board's social and political values."

A group of citizens called People Who Care met in April to discuss the growing controversy. The purpose of the organization was to remove "filthy" material from classrooms. One member expressed the group's general philosophy this way: "Children seek the parent to restrain them. A woman inherently seeks for man to be in authority over her and man seeks God to be in authority over him. It is not a question of equality . . . it is a required condition for a stable society." Another member stated the group's educational philosophy: "School decisions should be based on the absolutes of Christian behavior."

Bauer presented the Zykans' views in the United States District Court for the Northern District of Indiana. He claimed that the members of the Warsaw School Board had removed the controversial books because "words in the books offended [the board's] social, political, and moral tastes and not because the books, taken as a whole, were lacking in educational value." The board members had gotten rid of certain courses for similar reasons. Clearly, Bauer was relying on the *Right to Read* and *Minarcini* precedents to help him win his case.

Bauer also argued that the firing of Burnau and Dupont deprived students of the chance "to learn from and associate with these capable teachers." Additionally, it "created an . . . atmosphere of tension and fear . . . resulting in a . . . loss of academic freedom on the part of all teachers and students in the district." Bauer, of course, hoped that Indiana would interpret academic freedom as a First Amendment right—just as Mississippi had in the *Loewen* case.

Finally, Professor Bauer maintained that all the board's actions taken together violated students' "right to read" and "right to know." With these phrases he reminded the court of the Chelsea and Strongsville decisions. Certainly, it looked as if the plaintiffs had most of the precedents on their side.

But on December 3 the Indiana District Court refused to rule in the case of *Zykan v. Warsaw Community School Corp.* Judge Allen Sharp concluded that "he lacked jurisdiction over the subject matter." In other words, the judge felt that the school board had not violated anyone's constitutional rights.

Specifically, he said:

> The function of school officials is . . . to develop an opinion about what type of citizens are good citizens, to determine what curriculum and material will best develop good citizens, and to prohibit the use of texts, remove library books, and [drop] courses from the curriculum as a part of the effort to shape students into good citizens. And there is no way for school officials to make the [judgments] involved except on the basis of personal moral beliefs. To [claim] that school officials have made decisions . . . solely on the basis of personal "social, political, and moral" beliefs is insufficient to [show] a violation of constitutionally protected "academic freedom."

The plaintiffs appealed Judge Sharp's decision to the Seventh Circuit Court.

To improve the Zykan family's chances of winning on appeal, several organizations filed *amicus curiae* briefs. Again, these are documents submitted by "friends of the court" who are not directly involved in the case but are interested in its outcome. The groups were the Freedom to Read Foundation, the National Council of

Teachers of English, the Indiana Council of Teachers of English, the National Council for the Social Studies, the American Library Association, and the National Education Association.

Their briefs argued that the issues in the case were too serious to ignore. Schools should serve as forums for exchanging ideas, not as institutions for a "state-imposed orthodoxy." And "if the 'right to read and be exposed to controversial thoughts' cannot flourish anywhere in the school house, the prospects are bleak that it will ever flourish anywhere in society."

Elsewhere, the American Library Association has expressed its position in its "Freedom to Read Statement." Among other things, the ALA has said: "To some, much of modern literature is shocking. But is not much of life itself shocking? . . . Parents and teachers have a responsibility to prepare the young to meet the diversity of experiences in life to which they will be exposed, as they have a responsibility to help them learn to think critically for themselves. These are [positive] responsibilities, not to be [dismissed] simply by preventing them from reading works for which they are not yet prepared."

The school district argued that the case should be dismissed as "moot" or unjustified. The board members were merely following proper procedures. Indiana law required local boards to select new textbooks every five years. The district had decided to adopt a new English curriculum, and the old books simply did not fit into the new plans.

On August 22, 1980, Judge Walter J. Cummings of the Seventh Circuit Court agreed with part of the district court's conclusion. Like Judge Sharp, Judge Cummings felt that the school board had not violated anyone's constitutional rights. However, he also thought that the Zykans' charges were serious. So the plaintiffs would be allowed to amend their complaint, that is, to provide evidence of actual constitutional violations if they could find it.

In explaining his decision, Judge Cummings called the burning of *Values Clarification* a "[hateful] ceremony" that "no self-respecting citizen with a knowledge of history" could view calmly. He was probably referring to the fact that Nazi and other antidemocratic groups had burned books they disliked. But he noted that the book-burning incident had no real bearing on the legal issues in this case. On the other hand, the case was not moot because books had been removed and teachers had been fired.

The judge recognized that students *do* have constitutional rights. And he realized that other courts had interpreted the First Amendment to include academic freedom. But he gave two reasons why high school students should not have as much freedom as college students, for example.

First, high school students do not possess the same intellectual skills as older students. Therefore, they need more direction and guidance from their parents and teachers. Second, local residents have a vital interest in training young people who live in the community to be good neighbors and citizens. Therefore, state legislatures have given local school boards many powers to regulate high school classrooms. Judge Cummings cited the *Epperson* decision to support his point about state and local control of public education.

He went on to say that "the [scope] of these powers . . . reflects the [idea] that at the secondary school level the need for educational guidance [outweighs] . . . 'academic freedom.' . . . As a result, it is in general [proper] for local boards to make educational decisions based upon their personal social, political and moral views."

The judge also reminded board members that their authority is not absolute or unlimited. For example, school boards cannot fire teachers for making casual remarks in classrooms. Nor, according to the *Epperson* decision, can boards impose " 'a pall of orthodoxy.' " But the Zykan family failed to show that the Warsaw School Board had tried to force upon students any one specific point of view. And teachers who felt that they were fired unfairly should file their own separate lawsuits.

Finally, Judge Cummings explained that he based his decision on the *Presidents Council* precedent. Local boards *could* remove books that were considered obsolete, irrelevant, or improperly selected in the first place. And these were precisely the judgments that the Warsaw School Board had made about *Values Clarification, Growing Up Female in America, The Stepford Wives, Go Ask Alice,* and *The Bell Jar.*

The *Zykan* case resembled the *Right to Read, Minarcini, Loewen, Epperson,* and *Presidents Council* cases in ways that both Professor Bauer and Judge Cummings identified. The book-burning incident also recalled the disturbances in Kanawha County, though on a much smaller scale.

Like *Presidents Council, Zykan* was a need-to-protect win. The plaintiffs, the fired teachers, and the organizations that filed the *amicus curiae* briefs wanted students to know about nontraditional ways of thinking—especially feminism and ethical relativism. The school district and People Who Care wanted to shield students from nontraditional philosophies—especially ones that conflicted with some Christian ideas. The circuit court was closer to the need-to-protect groups than to the right-to-know groups. It said that school board members can change a district's curriculum as long as they don't force students to accept one point of view.

Zykan was important because it further strengthened a school board's authority to select and remove books. It also set limits on academic freedom for high school students. And it warned all those engaged in school book disputes that victories are always difficult to predict—no matter how favorable the precedents may seem to be.

The next chapter shows what another judge did when faced with the *Minarcini* and *Right to Read* precedents on the one hand and the *Presidents Council* and *Zykan* precedents on the other.

Chapter 7

Baileyville and the Vietnam War

American soldiers fought in Vietnam from 1965 to 1973. By the time the war ended in 1975, about 58,000 Americans had been killed and about 365,000 had been wounded. More than 1 million South Vietnamese soldiers lost their lives. And the number of deaths among North Vietnamese forces has been put at between 500,000 and 1 million. None of these figures includes the countless civilians who died.

The war left deep physical scars on the country of Vietnam. It also left deep emotional scars on the American families who lost friends and relatives in the Southeast Asian nation. Some people still have a hard time talking about the experience. And some parents in Baileyville, Maine, preferred that their children not read about the war's terrible realities.

Baileyville is located about one hundred miles northeast of Bangor. In 1981 it had a population of about 2,100. For such a small town, Baileyville had a lot of churches—four Protestant and one Catholic. The residents were mostly hard-working people employed at the Georgia-Pacific paper mills.

In April of 1981 Betsy Davenport—a fifteen-year-old ninth-grade student at Woodland High School—checked out a book about the Vietnam War from the school library. She got bored with it and passed it on to her friend Sandy Turner. Sandy's mother skimmed the book, then called Betsy's mother. Mrs. Turner asked Carol Ann Davenport if she knew that her stepdaughter had been reading a book with "dirty" words in it.

The book that Mrs. Turner and, eventually, Mrs. Davenport were upset about was *365 Days.* The title refers to the length of a military tour of duty in Vietnam. The book is a collection of realistic stories about American soldiers wounded during the war. It was written by Ronald Glasser, a doctor who treated those soldiers between 1968 and 1970.

365 Days was nominated for a National Book Award and was generally praised by reviewers. Thomas Lask of *The New York Times* called it "a book of great emotional impact." He identified Glasser's theme as "the waste of war, the destruction of our American young." In the *Saturday Review* Murray Polner wrote that the author "set out to relate simply and starkly what it meant to be a wounded and sometimes dying . . . combat trooper. . . . Not many better books on the horrors of war and its effect on individuals," Polner added, "have yet appeared."

However, when the book was performed as a play at the Kennedy Center in 1971, some people walked out of the performance. They were offended by the play's language and realistic descriptions of horrible injuries.

In 1982 Scott Campbell wrote a detailed article for *Northeast Magazine* called "Banned in Baileyville." He reported:

There are a total of 452 words in the book which might be considered objectionable by one person or another. About 40 per cent of them are "dirty," having mostly to do with body parts and functions. The other 60 per cent or so are to do with the loss of those body parts and functions, often by a violent and unspeakably painful death. Many of the "dirty" words were spoken by 18- and 19-year-olds who had just awakened, for instance, to find that both their legs were missing.

Carol Ann Davenport objected to *365 Days* because "it would be just as good a story without using all that language. I don't think any writing," she said, "needs to include four-letter words." Mrs. Davenport took her objections to her Baptist minister, Roy Blevins; the chairman of the school committee, Thomas Golden; a committee member, Clifford McPhee; and the Superintendent of Schools Raymond Freve. She wanted the book removed from the school library.

At the April 28, 1981, meeting of the school committee, Superintendent Freve distributed photocopies of parts of one chapter. He read some favorable reviews of the book out loud. Then he suggested that *365 Days* be put on the library's restricted shelf until all the committee members could read the entire work. But after a brief discussion, the committee voted five to zero to remove the book and ban it from school property, including school buses. Chairman Golden later explained that *365 Days* was banned not because it dealt with the Vietnam War, but because of its "offensive and abusive" language.

When the book's publisher heard about the committee's action, the managing editor wrote to Golden: "I would ask you to reconsider your decision for the sake of your students, the ideals of education and knowledge, and also the freedoms of speech and thought. We shall not be protecting our youth if we [wrap] them in ignorance, nor shall we earn or deserve their respect, if we cannot place enough trust and faith in them to reason and respond on their own behalves."

The president of the Authors League of America also wrote to the committee chairman: "Each book banning by a school board increases the tide of suppression that threatens the freedoms of the First Amendment. . . . Offensive language in books does not hurt high school students, but a restriction of their freedom to read will injure them." Golden's reaction to the two letters was: "We're here trying to do what we hope is best for the children."

At the May 5 committee meeting, Michael Sheck—an eighteen-year-old senior who had already read *365 Days*—asked the members to lift their ban. They refused. So on the day of the next meeting, Sheck drove one hundred miles to Bangor to get a copy of the book. He planned to show it to other students. However, Woodland Principal John Morrison stopped Sheck in the hallway and told him to get the book off school property.

More than fifty people attended the evening committee meeting. The student council reported that it had voted unanimously for the return of *365 Days* to the school library. A Methodist minister read a passage from the Bible that included some of the same "dirty" words the committee was censoring. But committee member McPhee said: "I work at the mill, and I hear people using that language all the time—and their kids. The kids already know the words, but the school shouldn't say it's right." And Reverend Blevins commented: "I don't see it as banning but as selectivity of education." By a vote of three to two, the school committee decided to keep the book off the library shelf.

On June 17, at Superintendent Freve's suggestion, the committee agreed to draw up a policy for handling complaints about books. Two committee members moved that *365 Days* be put on the restricted shelf until the policy was established. Michael Sheck warned the school committee that he would file a lawsuit if this motion did not pass. Afterwards he explained: "The chance there might be one person who wanted to read that book and didn't get the chance to is what frightened me." Freve pointed out that no one would be likely to check out the book over summer vacation. So the committee members voted three to two to make the book available to students with parental permission to read it.

During the summer of 1981, Sheck received several threatening phone calls and some hate mail. One of the letters used two of the "dirty" words that people objected to in *365 Days*. The letter was signed "A Concerned Christian." But he also got mail supporting his stand. One Vietnam veteran wrote: "Don't let them stop us from telling our story just because of the words we had to use to tell it."

On August 17 the school committee members adopted a policy for dealing with book complaints. However, the majority voted *against* applying the policy to *365 Days* and *for* banning the book entirely. Chairman Golden said: "It's just that *365 Days* had too much gross language. I think there's a lot better books on war. Books like *The Red Badge of Courage* or *All Quiet on the Western Front*. Maybe I've heard some of these offensive words, but I sure don't use them as part of my vocabulary and I don't like to be around people who use them."

Sheck decided to sue. On Stepember 3 he named Golden, Freve, McPhee, and one other committee member as defendants. The suit charged them with violating students' First and Fourteenth Amendment rights and sought a preliminary injunction to put *365 Days* back on the high school library's shelf. The book's publisher, the Authors League of America, the Maine Library Association, and the Maine Teachers Association each filed *amicus curiae* briefs for the plaintiffs.

The case of *Sheck* v. *Baileyville School Committee* was tried just before Christmas in the United States District Court at Bangor. Before the hearings started, a small group of Vietnam veterans gathered on the courthouse steps. One former soldier carried an American flag. The others held handmade signs. Some of the signs read: "Censor War, Not History." "War is the Only Obscenity," and "The Moral Majority Sent Us There, Now Let Them Listen to What Happened."

Judge Conrad K. Cyr presided over the hearings. His first instruction to the attorneys was that none of the language in question could be used in court. The main term that people were upset about was a four-letter word for sexual intercourse. Judge Cyr told the lawyers to refer to this term as "the word." Other objectionable terms would be refered to as "the s-word," "the b-word," and so on.

Ronald R. Coles, an attorney for the Maine Civil Liberties Union, represented Michael Sheck. Coles called Carol Ann Davenport to the witness stand. He read her passages from unidentified books. Then he asked her if she would favor removing those books from the library. She said she would. Coles identified the passages as taken from *Ulysses* by James Joyce and *The Merchant of Venice* by William Shakespeare.

The lawyer also asked the witness whether she had ever used any of the language she objected to in *365 Days.* She said she never had. Coles then called John Boyce, one of Mrs. Davenport's ex-husbands. Mr. Boyce testified that Carol Ann had "a general vocabulary of several four-letter words." She had used these words often, he said, especially during the last six months of their marriage and in front of their children.

Dr. Glasser and other writers about the Vietnam War testified that the four-letter words were necessary to tell the story accurately.

Glasser explained that one of his patients had screamed in pain for seven full days. The patient had *not* used expressions like "golly gee." A Vietnam veteran said on the stand: "The very fact that those words exist in that book brings into reality the smell and the feelings and the noise and the horrors. . . . Removal of those words would remove the very essence . . . [would] take away, in fact, the horrors that existed."

Coles asked the head of the Woodland High School English Department if she thought the language in *365 Days* would harm students. She answered: "Well, if they are corrupted by words, they couldn't have had much moral fiber to begin with." The school librarian testified that many other books in the school library used the same language.

Michael Sheck said that he heard his fellow students use " 'the word' at least once a day." Another student testified that the school didn't teach much about the Vietnam War, and *365 Days* had given her a new view of it.

Principal Morrison admitted that he had reminded teachers involved in the controversy not to forget who paid them. But he said he had only been joking. Defendant McPhee commented that "the school committee should have the right to set the standards for that school and what they're going to allow in that school."

Daniel L. Lacasse represented the Baileyville School Committee. He cross-examined Coles's witnesses but didn't call any of his own. He mainly presented several arguments to the judge:

- The committee's removal of *365 Days* was not intended to limit free speech.

- Students could get the book elsewhere; therefore, they would not suffer "irreparable injury" because of the committee's action.

- Various precedents said that a judge should stay out of local school matters unless constitutional issues were at stake.

- No constitutional issues were at stake in this case.

On January 22, 1982, Judge Cyr delivered his opinion in *Sheck* v. *Baileyville School Committee.* He decided that even though the committee did not *intend* to limit free speech, constitutional issues *were* at stake. "The information and ideas in books placed in a school library," he said "are protected speech and the First Amendment right of students to receive that information and those ideas is entitled to constitutional protection."

He also decided that Sheck and his fellow plaintiffs *would* suffer "irreparable injury" if *365 Days* were not put back on the school library's shelf. He cited a precedent that stated: "It is well established that the loss of First Amendment freedoms constitutes irreparable injury."

The judge then discussed other precedents. On the one hand, the *Minarcini* and *Right to Read* cases declared that students have a right to "be exposed to controversial thoughts and language." On the other hand, the *Presidents Council* case said that school boards can remove library books. And the *Zykan* case indicated that book-banning might not violate high school students' right to academic freedom.

Judge Cyr came down on the side of *Minarcini* and *Right to Read.* He too saw high school libraries as "marketplaces of ideas." And he concluded that "First Amendment rights must be [granted to] all 'persons' in the market for ideas, including secondary school students."

It did not matter that the school committee only objected to the language in *365 Days.* For "as long as words convey ideas," the judge noted, "federal courts must remain on First Amendment alert in book banning cases. . . . A less vigilant rule would leave the care of the flock to the fox that is only after their feathers." Also, the committee offered no evidence that coarse language would harm students in any way.

On the due process issue, Judge Cyr said that "a book may not be banned from a public school library in disregard of the requirements of the Fourteenth Amendment." He cited the Mississippi rating committee's actions in the *Loewen* case as examples of failure to follow due process. He also criticized the Baileyville School Committee for failing to apply its own policy on book complaints to *365 Days.*

Because the *Sheck* decision followed the *Minarcini* and *Right to Read* precedents, it was a right-to-know victory. The plaintiffs and the groups that filed the *amicus curiae* briefs wanted students to understand the realities of the Vietnam War, even if those realities included four-letter words. The defendants wanted to protect students from "offensive and abusive" language. But unlike the Indiana Circuit Court in the *Zykan* case, the Maine District Court took a strong stand in favor of high school students' First Amendment rights.

The Baileyville School Committee seriously considered appealing Judge Cyr's decision. However, the committee members wanted to see how the Supreme Court would rule in another school book battle that had erupted in New York. The next chapter explains what happened in that landmark case.

Chapter 8

Raid on the Island Trees Library

On the night of November 7, 1975, Island Trees Union Free School District No. 26 was holding a sports festival. Two school board members who were attending the festival left early. They went to the nearby high school and got the night janitor to let them into the library. There they searched the card catalog for books that appeared on a list of "objectionable" works. The board members found nine books that they considered "mentally dangerous."

The Island Trees School District is located in Levittown, just outside of New York City. Levittown is one of many suburbs that sprang up quickly across the nation after World War II. During the mid-seventies its residents were mainly white, middle-class Catholics of Irish or Italian descent. They tended to be conservative on most social issues.

In February of 1976 the seven-member Island Trees School

Board held one of its regular meetings. After the public meeting, the board members had a private meeting with the district's two high school principals. The principals were shown quotations from the nine "objectionable" books. They were told to remove the works from the library shelves. And they were asked to look for other books on the board's list. Soon the principals located a tenth book at a junior high school in the district. An eleventh book was later found on the reading list for a senior literature course.

The superintendent of schools objected to the board's decision to ban the works without a review committee hearing. But on March 3 the board president issued an order to the superindent. The order directed him to remove "*all* copies of the library books" immediately.

The eleven books that the school board banned included four novels—*A Hero Ain't Nothin' But a Sandwich* by Alice Childress, *Slaughterhouse Five* by Kurt Vonnegut, Jr., *Laughing Boy* by Oliver La Farge, and *The Fixer* by Bernard Malamud. The last two had both won Pulitzer Prizes for literature. Three of the eleven were autobiographies—*Down These Mean Streets* by Piri Thomas, *Black Boy* by Richard Wright, and *Go Ask Alice* by an unknown teenager. Two were nonfiction works—one on animal behavior, *The Naked Ape* by Desmond Morris, and one on social conditions, *Soul on Ice* by Eldridge Cleaver. Two were anthologies or collections of stories— *A Reader for Writers* edited by Jerome W. Archer and Joseph Schwartz and *Best Short Stories by Negro Writers* edited by Langston Hughes.

The New York Civil Liberties Union threatened to take legal action against the Island Trees School Board. Barbara Bernstein of the NYCLU described the banned books as being "about blacks, about ghetto life, about the physiology of sex, about the effects of racial and religious hatred and hypocrisy—all aspects of life which young people need to know about." The liberal organization sent the board members a letter. Part of it said: "While you may consider the content of the books to be unpopular, offensive or representative of only a minority viewpoint, nevertheless, the history and spirit of the First Amendment has been not merely to tolerate but to encourage dissenting views." The board vowed to defend itself against any legal action and called a press conference to explain its position.

At the March 19 press conference the board issued a statement saying that three board members had attended a meeting back in September of 1975. The meeting was sponsored by Parents of New York–United. (PONY–U was a conservative group concerned with educational issues; it had participated in the Kanawha County book controversy.) At the September meeting the board members had obtained their list of "objectionable" books. The works were described as "anti-American, anti-Christian, anti-Semitic, and just plain filthy." This PONY–U list of books inspired the raid on the library. However, the board members did not think of themselves as "book banners" or "book burners." Most of them agreed that the works did belong in public libraries. However they all agreed that the books did *not* belong in school libraries.

Shortly after the press conference, the school board mailed out a special edition of its newsletter. The edition raised these questions: "Does the news media decide from which books your children are taught? Should it be the people who award the Pulitzer prizes? Or, maybe it should be today's dedicated teacher union leaders?" The board's newsletter concluded: "We believe that not even the professional educators and educational administrators have a right to [take away] the parents' authority. . . . God help all of us if the parents should ever lose this authority." A teachers' union leader pointed out that the board had approved the books for purchase and was now "violating its own procedures."

On March 30, 1976, the school board agreed to appoint four Island Trees residents and four district employees to review the books. The residents were a recently graduated high school student, a former board president, a former PTA president, and a mailman. The employees were an English teacher, a social studies teacher, a high school principal, and an elementary school principal.

By July 1 the review committee recommended that four books be returned to the school libraries—*Laughing Boy, Black Boy, Go Ask Alice,* and *Best Short Stories by Negro Writers.* The committee also recommended that *Slaughterhouse Five* and *The Fixer* be returned but lent only to students with parental permission. *The Naked Ape* and *Down These Mean Streets* should be removed. However, the committee members could not agree on *A Hero Ain't Nothin' But a Sandwich, A Reader for Writers,* and *Soul on Ice.*

The board took little of the committee's advice. It voted to return *Laughing Boy* and, on a restricted basis, *Black Boy.* Otherwise, it decided to ban the remaining nine books. President Richard Ahrens said that the board would not "answer any questions on the merits of the books. . . . It is not only our right but our duty to make the decision," he explained, "and we would do it again in the face of the abuse heaped upon us by the media."

The Island Trees School District is in the Second Circuit where the *Presidents Council* case was decided. But in August the Sixth Circuit Court of Appeals ruled in the *Minarcini* case. The NYCLU felt that the *Minarcini* decision might resolve the differences of opinion between the two circuits. So the civil liberties organization helped Steven Pico and four other students prepare a case against the Island Trees Board.

On January 4, 1977, Pico and his fellow plaintiffs filed a class-action lawsuit for all the students in the district. The suit charged the school board with violating the constitutional rights of students and the academic freedom rights of librarians and teachers. Specifically, the plaintiffs argued that their First Amendment right to be free of "the pall of orthodoxy" had been violated. And the NYCLU argued that the board had banned the nine books for political, not educational, reasons. The New York Library Association, the Association of American Publishers, and twenty-two other groups filed *amicus curiae* briefs in support of the plaintiffs.

The lawyer for the school board responded to the lawsuit by mailing out a questionnaire to 4,979 homes in the district. The questionnaire asked residents whether they supported the board's removal of the books. Out of the 866 people who replied, 508 (or 59 percent) said yes and 358 (or 41 percent) said no. In arguing the case itself, the board maintained that it had unlimited power to protect traditional ideas of right and wrong and to teach students those ideas. The board also argued that it had banned the books for educational, not political, reasons.

The case of *Pico v. Board of Education, Island Trees Union Free School District* was decided more than two-and-a-half years after the suit had been filed. District Court Judge George C. Pratt denied a trial and ruled in favor of the board. Judge Pratt concluded that the board had not directly and sharply violated anyone's First Amendments rights. It had removed the books for conservative educational reasons. Therefore, the *Presidents Council* precedent required a judgment for the board. Besides, Judge Edwards in the *Minarcini* case had misinterpreted the *Presidents Council* case. Pico appealed Pratt's decision to the next highest court.

On October 2, 1980, the three-judge Second Circuit Court of Appeals voted two to one in favor of the students. It reversed the district court's decision and ordered that a trial be held. The purpose of the trial would be to discover the school board's *real* reasons for banning the nine books.

Judge Charles P. Sifton wrote the majority opinion. He said that the *Presidents Council* precedent did not apply to this case because the facts were different. There was no reason to suspect the community board's motives for removing *Down These Mean Streets* in the 1972 conflict. "In this case, however," Judge Sifton observed, "what we have instead is an unusual and irregular intervention in the school libraries' operations by persons not routinely concerned with such matters." So the board's motives could have been "to express an official policy with regard to God and country."

Judge Jon O. Newman agreed with Sifton. The students had shown that their First Amendment rights *might* have been violated. But only a trial could *prove* a constitutional violation. Judge Newman said that the board members' actions would be unconstitutional even if their motives were only partly political. And he noted that "there are few legitimate reasons why a book . . . should be removed from a library not filled to capacity."

Judge Walter R. Mansfield disagreed with the other two judges. He felt that the *Pico* case was just like the *Presidents Council* case. He described the Sixth Circuit Court's reasoning in *Minarcini* as "logically flawed." And he quoted the Seventh Circuit Court's opinion in the *Zykan* case: school boards *could* base educational decisions on "their personal social, political and moral views." So he concluded that the "court should keep its hands off" board actions. But since Judge Mansfield's opinion was a minority view, the Island Trees School Board appealed the majority ruling to the United States Supreme Court.

The Supreme Court agreed to hear the case because of the differences of opinion in the lower courts. Oral arguments were presented on March 2, 1982. Attorney George W. Lipp, Jr., spoke for the board. He maintained that federal courts should not interfere with school boards' decisions. The Island Trees School Board had decided that the nine books contained "indecent matter, vulgarities, profanities, [clear] descriptions of sexual relations, [and] some [insulting] remarks about blacks, Jews, or Christ." The books were available elsewhere and, therefore, the board's ban did not violate anyone's First Amendment rights.

Alan H. Levine of the NYCLU represented the students. He argued that the Island Trees School Board did not remove any other school library books that contained the same language. Therefore, the board members must have had special reasons for removing *these* books. A trial should be held to determine if the board's reasons were political. "All we are saying," Levine declared, "is that there are some limits to what they can do in the name of their values. . . . While schools do transmit values, they may not ignore their obligation to respect diversity."

The Supreme Court decided the case on June 25. By a vote of five to four, the Court ruled in favor of the students. It ordered that the case be sent back to the district court for a trial.

Four of the five majority justices agreed on the First Amendment issues at stake. If the board banned the books because they expressed unpopular ideas, then the board violated students' First Amendment rights. If the board removed the books because they were "educationally unsuitable," then the board did not violate students' rights. The fifth majority justice refused to rule on First Amendment questions without more facts. The four minority justices said that the issues in the case were matters for local authorities, not federal judges, to decide.

Justice William J. Brennan, Jr., wrote the majority opinion. He spoke for Justices Marshall and Stevens when he said: "We think that the First Amendment rights of students may be directly and sharply [violated] by the removal of books from the shelves of a school library. . . . In keeping with this principle, we have held that . . . 'the Constitution protects the right to receive information and ideas.' " He noted the board's concern about the "anti-American" ideas in some of the books. And he felt that this concern raised questions about the board's political motives that only a trial could answer. "In brief," Justice Brennan concluded, "we hold that local school boards may not remove books from school library shelves simply because they dislike the ideas contained in those books."

Chief Justice Warren E. Burger wrote the main dissenting opinion. He feared that the majority ruling would turn the Supreme Court into a "super censor" of school board library decisions. "In order to fulfill its function," Justice Burger reasoned, "an elected school board *must* express its views on the subjects which are taught to its students. In doing so those elected officials express the views of their community; they may err, of course, and the voters may remove them."

The Supreme Court ruling in the *Pico* case was a win for the right to know. The plaintiffs, the NYCLU, and the groups that filed the *amicus curiae* briefs wanted students to learn about ideas that differed from the community's. The school board members wanted to protect students from ideas that the board considered "educationally unsuitable." But the Court's decision was far from a resounding right-to-know victory. The almost equal split between the nine justices mirrored the deep split between various educational pressure groups.

After the *Pico* ruling the Baileyville School Committee voted not to appeal Judge Cyr's decision in favor of Michael Sheck and *365 Days*. The committee members felt that they would probably lose such an appeal. On August 12, 1982, the Island Trees School Board voted not to go to trial. A board representative explained that a trial "would have the effect of surrendering local control of the schools to the courts."

The board members agreed to return all nine books to the district's school libraries. However, they also told librarians to send notices to the parents of students who checked out any of the books. A sample notice read: "The Board of Education wishes to inform you that the book(s) selected by your child may contain materials which you may find objectionable."

The NYCLU challenged this policy. And in December of 1982, the New York State Attorney General's office told the Island Trees School Board to remove its red "Parental Notification" stamps from the nine books. The Attorney General said that the board's policy violated the state's law guaranteeing the privacy of all library records.

The U.S. Supreme Court had finally decided a school censorship case. But school book disputes rage on. The following chapter and the postscript show that some of these battles have returned to the issues raised in the Kanawha County war.

Chapter 9

The Learning Tree in Washington

He thought, "What are grasshoppers for anyway, and snakes and mosquitoes and flies and worms, wasps, potato bugs and things? Seems they ain't much good to the world, but God put 'em here. Seems they got as much rights as we have to live. If the grasshoppers didn't eat the crops, they'd starve. No worse'n us killin' hogs and chickens so we don't go hungry. Hogs and chickens and cows and rabbits and squirrels, possums and such must hate us much as we hate mosquitoes and gnats and flies. Dogs and cats and horses are 'bout the luckiest. 'Bout the only ones we don't go round killin' off all the time. The Ten Commandments say we oughtn't kill, then we come home from church and wring a chicken's neck for dinner—and Reverend Broadnap eats more'n anybody else." Newt stretched. "Too much for me to figger out," he said aloud.

T his passage from *The Learning Tree* was one of fifteen passages that the plaintiffs objected to in *Grove v. Mead School District No. 354.* The book is an autobiographical novel about a black family living in a small Kansas town during the 1920s. It was written by Gordon Parks, a famous photographer, and was published by Harper & Row in 1963. Newt Winger is the main character. The book centers on his teenaged experiences with sex, the town bully, and the problem of death.

Several reviewers liked the novel. At least one recommended it for adolescent readers. Nat Hentoff, writing for *New York Herald Tribune Books,* commented: "*The Learning Tree* should be placed on high school reading lists, including those in schools in 'disadvantaged' neighborhoods. White youngsters have much to learn from this tree, and Negro boys will be able to identify much more strongly and hopefully with Newt Winger's story than they can with many books about alien American experiences which they are now required to read." However, the reviewer for *The New Yorker* warned: "At the end, the reader's head swirls with an accumulation of brutal murders, dismemberments, fist fights, automobile accidents, beatings, . . . and blood, blood, blood."

In April of 1980 Cassie Grove was assigned the novel in her sophomore English class. She was enrolled at Mead High School in the state of Washington. Cassie read part of the book and found it offensive to her religious beliefs. She showed the novel to her mother. Mrs. Grove read the whole book and also found it offensive. She told her daughter's teacher about their objections. Cassie was assigned another novel and given permission to leave the room during discussions of *The Learning Tree.* However, she decided to stay.

Mrs. Grove then filed a formal complaint against the book. A school district evaluation committee reviewed the novel. The committee members found it to be "an appropriate element in the sophomore English curriculum." The Grove family appealed this decision. But the district's board of directors refused to remove the book from the second-year reading list.

On December 31, 1980, attorney Michael P. Farris filed a lawsuit for the Groves in the United States District Court for the Eastern District of Washington. His suit charged that use of *The Learning Tree* violated the religion clauses of the First Amendment. "Those clauses provide that 'Congress shall make no law respecting an establishment of religion, or prohibiting the free exercise thereof.' " In 1980 Farris was the General Legal Counsel for the Moral Majority of Washington State.

The Moral Majority is a conservative political organization. It was founded in 1979 by the Reverend Jerry Falwell, a Baptist minister from Lynchburg, Virginia. Among other things, members of the Moral Majority support voluntary prayer in public schools, strong national defense policies, and strict laws against pornography and drug abuse. They oppose legalized abortion and civil rights for homosexuals.

Before the case came to trial, Farris explained his clients' position at the American Library Association's 1981 Annual Conference:

The Mead case involves a public school textbook called *The Learning Tree*—and its a *textbook*, not a library book, that we're concerned about. I would not be concerned at all if the book . . . were on the library shelves of Mead High School or any other high school around this country. I think it's an appropriate book in a voluntary setting. But when it becomes a required text it must be seen in a different light and from a different legal perspective.

In the non-jury trial the plaintiffs maintained that the novel violated their free exercise of religion by establishing a competing religion called "secular humanism." Much of the debate in the case revolved around two questions. How should secular humanism be defined? And, is it really a religion? Farris defined secular humanism as "a religion dedicated to . . . opposing or showing hostility toward Christianity." He also argued that "it has declared its pulpit to be the public school classroom and its 'bible' is adolescent literature like *The Learning Tree.*"

Actually, the controversy over secular humanism dates back to the 1960s. Max Rafferty, California's superintendent of public instruction, was criticized for the state's failure to educate. In 1969 he issued a report that blamed "humanists for progressive education, promoting birth control, materialism, abandoning absolute ethical and moral standards, infiltrating the U.S. Supreme Court, replacing religion with science, and [too much] sexual [freedom]."

According to the editors of a book called *The First Freedom Today,* "opposition to secular humanism had become a key plank in the platform of the Moral Majority" during the 1980 presidential campaign. And according to *Newsweek* magazine, "the preacher-politicians of the Moral Majority [changed] the terms 'liberal' and 'liberalism' into synonyms for godlessness and immorality. Now . . . the fundamentalist New Right," *Newsweek* continued, "has shifted its [terms] and tactics to confront a new bogyman. The target is what Christian fundamentalists label 'humanism.' "

On September 27, 1982, the U.S. District Court decided the case of *Grove* v. *Mead School District No. 354.* Judge Robert J. McNichols ruled in favor of the defendant district. He said that the plaintiffs had failed to state a cause of action. In other words, the Grove family had failed to show that *The Learning Tree* created a legal problem which the court should solve. The family then took its case to the Ninth Circuit Court of Appeals.

On February 22, 1985, the appellate court agreed with the district court. Judge Eugene A. Wright wrote the majority opinion. He found that the school district did not violate the free exercise clause of the First Amendment. He also held that use of *The Learning Tree* did not constitute establishment of religion.

Judge Wright gave several reasons for his position. Cassie Grove had not been forced to read the novel. As soon as the Grove family objected to *The Learning Tree,* Cassie had been assigned another book. She had been excused from class discussions about the novel. But she freely chose to stay. *The Learning Tree* was one of many religiously neutral books in the sophomore English course. In other words, the Parks book neither supported nor opposed any religion. It simply described the lives and thoughts of certain black Americans.

The judge commented: "The state interest in providing well-rounded public education would be critically [blocked] by [the granting] of Grove's wishes." And he quoted from a precedent which said: "If we are to eliminate everything that is objectionable to any of the [the religious bodies existing in the United States], . . . we will leave public education in shreds." However, Judge Wright admitted that "secular humanism may be a religion."

Judge William C. Canby, Jr., wrote a concurring opinion. He agreed with Judge Wright's decision about the novel. But he discussed the conflict between Christian fundamentalism and secular humanism much more deeply.

In his remarks on the establishment clause, Judge Canby quoted from precedents which said: " 'One of the [requirements] of the First Amendment is to promote a . . . pluralistic society and to keep government neutral . . . between believers and nonbelievers.' Neutrality is designed to protect religion as well as government. 'A union of government and religion tends to destroy government and to degrade religion.' "

On the specific question of whether secular hunanism is a religion, the judge answered no. He admitted that some humanists might be religious. But he described secular humanism as a philosophy that does not necessarily include belief in a supreme being or in anything supernatural. In fact, what Judge Canby felt the plaintiffs were really concerned about was the public school curriculum in general and *The Learning Tree* in particular. They seemed to fear that both the courses and the book were just too "secular" or "worldly."

The judge assumed that *The Learning Tree* did express some anti-Christian ideas. He also assumed that these ideas did offend the Grove family. But the crucial issue was whether use of the novel meant that school officials (government representatives) endorsed, supported, or approved of these ideas. Again Judge Canby answered no.

In explaining his answer, the judge noted that the passages the plaintiffs disliked were simply a fictional character's thoughts on questions of evil and suffering. These thoughts, he said, are "bound to be understood by Cassie Grove's classmates—high school sophomores confronting many of the same questions, and doubtless beginning to appreciate that many of the comforting [ideas] of childhood are not always what they seemed." Judge Canby concluded that posing disturbing questions is not the same as forcing people to accept anti-religious ideas.

Finally, the judge observed that "while [the free exercise clause] protects individuals from governmental interference with their religion, . . . it does not protect the individual from being religiously offended by what the government does." And he quoted from the Supreme Court's ruling in the *Pico* case: "Our Constitution does not permit the official suppression of ideas."

Attorney Farris called the *Grove* decision "a grave defeat for civil liberties." He appealed his case to the Supreme Court. But on October 7, 1985, the Court refused to review the matter.

The *Grove* decision was another win for the right to know. The plaintiffs and the Moral Majority wanted to protect students from anti-Christian ideas. The defendants wanted students to appreciate the realities of growing up black in America, even if those realities conflicted with fundamentalist beliefs about right and wrong.

The school book battle in Mead, Washington, was most like the war in Kanawha County. Both controversies pitted parents against school officials. The parents saw certain books as anti-religious. The officials saw those same books as valuable sources of knowledge about the modern world.

Unlike the West Virginia war, the Washington state battle ended not in a draw but in a clear-cut, right-to-know victory. And the Grove family identified not merely a book and a publisher as the enemy but a philosophy of education called secular humanism.

The postscript shows that court cases between fundamentalists and humanists have become the main book battles of the 1980s.

Postscript:
Southern Fundamentalists and
Secular Humanists

At the end of the 1925 Scopes "monkey trial," the famous journalist H. L. Mencken made this comment: "The fire is still burning on a far-flung hill, and it may begin to roar again at any moment." As of 1987 several fires were roaring in Tennessee, Alabama, and Louisiana.

In Tennessee Christian fundamentalists and school officials continue to wage a battle that began in 1983. On May 12 of that year, the school district for Church Hill, Tennessee, adopted a reading series for kindergarten through eighth grade. The series, published by Holt, Rinehart and Winston, had been used by nearly 10 million children across the nation for a decade.

One Tennessee mother, Vicki Frost, felt that the sixth-grade reader offended her religious beliefs. So on September 1 she helped organize a meeting at the Church Hill Middle School. The purpose of the meeting was to bring like-minded citizens together.

Mrs. Frost and other parents formed Citizens Organized for Better Schools (COBS). The group got written criticisms of the Holt series from Mel and Norma Gabler, the same Texas couple who had participated in the Kanawha County conflict. COBS then petitioned the Hawkins County School Board to remove all the readers from the district's classrooms. The parents also asked the board to provide other books and reading classes suitable for their fundamentalist children.

The principal of the Church Hill Middle School did briefly offer alternative classes. But the principal of Carter's Valley Elementary School did not. And different groups formed to fight COBS. Citizens Advocating the Right to Education (CARE) included non-fundamentalist parents, teachers, and religious leaders and was determined to "defend the educational system of America . . . from disruption and censorship." Non-fundamentalist students formed the Church Hill Ministerial Association.

On November 10 the school board unanimously passed a district-wide resolution. The directive told teachers to "use only textbooks adopted by the Board of Education as regular classroom textbooks." The Church Hill Middle School stopped providing alternative reading classes.

Mrs. Frost went to the Church Hill Elementary School where one of her children was attending second grade. She took her daughter out of class and began teaching the girl reading in the school library. Frost refused to leave the grounds and was charged with trespassing. She sued for false arrest and eventually won a $70,000 judgment.

After the Church Hill Elementary School incident, ten fundamentalist children refused to read the Holt books. The children were suspended. Several of them enrolled in private Christian schools.

On December 3 the Mozert family and eleven other fundamentalist families filed a lawsuit against the Hawkins County Public

Schools in the United States District Court for the Eastern District of Tennessee. The plaintiffs claimed that the Holt series:

1. Teaches witchcraft and other forms of magic
2. Teaches that right and wrong vary from situation to situation
3. Teaches children to disobey and not respect their parents
4. Shows prayer to an idol
5. Teaches that people do not need to believe in God in a specific way but that any type of faith in the supernatural is an acceptable method of salvation
6. Shows a child who does not respect his mother's Bible study
7. Implies that Jesus could not read or write
8. Teaches that man and apes evolved from a common ancestor
9. Teaches secular humanism

The fundamentalists also charged that the school officials' refusal to remove the Holt readers and to provide other books violated the free exercise clause of the First Amendment. And, in a new twist for school book battles; the parents asked that their children be allowed to "opt out" of classes where the *Holt Basic Readers* were used. In other words, if the officials would not remove the books from the schools, then the families would remove the children from the classes.

The plaintiffs were represented by Michael P. Farris, the same attorney who had represented the Groves in *The Learning Tree* case. By this time, Farris was also serving as the legal counsel for a conservative organization called Concerned Women for America. The conservative group helped the plaintiffs. And People for the American Way—a liberal organization founded by television producer Norman Lear—helped the defendants.

On February 24, 1984, District Court Judge Thomas G. Hull dismissed the suit—except for claim 5. But he pointed out: "Only if the plaintiffs can prove that the books . . . are teaching a particular religious faith as true, . . . or teaching that the students must be saved through some religious pathway, or that no salvation is required, can . . . mere exposure to these books [be considered] a violation of free exercise rights." So the judge told the plaintiffs to submit passages from the books that would prove their claim.

About two weeks later attorney Farris submitted a "Memorandum Regarding Stories on Issue of Salvation." He cited an essay by a vice president at Holt, Rinehart and Winston that favorably mentioned a "world community." Farris maintained: "Those who cling to Judeo-Christianity reject the whole concept of world-community, one-world-government, or human interdependency." He then discussed a poem called "The Blind Men and the Elephant" and a passage from *The Diary of Anne Frank.* The lawyer argued that these selections could give children the idea that all religions are the same or equal—an idea which fundamentalists also reject.

After reading Farris's memorandum, Judge Hull dismissed claim 5 and granted summary judgment in favor of the defendant school district. He concluded that the Holt books were religiously neutral. They did not teach children religion, nor did they try to get children to give up religion.

Farris appealed Hull's decision in *Mozert* v. *Hawkins County Public Schools* to the United States Court of Appeals for the Sixth Circuit. The appellate court reversed the district court's ruling. The judges of the Sixth Circuit felt that only a trial could answer some lingering questions. For example, were the fundamentalists sincere in their beliefs? And, would the parents' "opt-out" request interfere with the district's reading program?

The July 1985 non-jury trial became known as "Scopes II." On the witness stand Vicki Frost objected to a Holt book that described chimpanzees as man's "closest relative." She disapproved of Cinderella, King Arthur, and Wizard of Oz stories because they contained magic, good witches, and supernatural acts. She complained about readings that reversed traditional male and female roles. And she was offended by stories that criticized the American way of doing business because "capitalism is ordained by God."

A lawyer for the school district remarked: "Lift the petticoat and look underneath, and it's just censorship." But attorney Farris replied: "How can people call this a censorship case? If we win, there will be more books, not fewer. It's Scopes in reverse."

Judge Hull rendered his third decision on October 24, 1986. He found that the fundamentalists were sincere in their beliefs. Therefore, the plaintiffs were "entitled to protection under the Free Exercise Clause of the First Amendment." The judge noted that Cassie Grove had been assigned alternative reading and excused from class discussions of *The Learning Tree* in the Washington case. So he found that the Tennessee fundamentalists' "opt-out" request would not interfere with the Hawkins County reading program.

But Judge Hull also ordered the Church Hill parents to teach their children reading at home. And the fundamentalists had to convince school officials that the children were learning the same skills as students in regular reading classes. Finally, he awarded seven families a total of about $50,000 to cover the expenses they had incurred while sending their children to private schools. As of mid–1987 the defendant school district was preparing to appeal Hull's third decision to the United States Supreme Court.

Meanwhile, in Alabama, 624 Christian fundamentalist parents, teachers, and students sued the school commissioners of Mobile County. Their suit asked that all traces of secular humanism be removed from the schools' curricula.

The case of *Smith* v. *Board of School Commissioners of Mobile County* actually grew out of a 1982 case in which U.S.

District Court Judge W. Brevard Hand had contradicted several landmark Supreme Court rulings. In the 1982 dispute Judge Hand had upheld two Alabama laws permitting prayer in public schools. He had also ruled that the First Amendment did not apply to the states in such cases. The Eleventh Circuit Court of Appeals reversed the judge. But he restructured the issue to allow the fundamentalists to challenge forty-five textbooks in the county school system. The issue in the *Smith* case was whether the books illegally taught a religion called secular humanism which, according to the plaintiffs, puts human beings above God.

Former Alabama Governor George Wallace, the Concerned Women for America, the Gablers, and the National Legal Foundation (formed by television preacher Pat Robertson) sided with the fundamentalists. The executive director of the NLF, Robert Skolrood, called the confrontation "one of the most important trials of the last several decades." People for the American Way provided legal help for the board. The president of PAW, Anthony T. Podesta, said that the suit was a "hoax [produced] by people who don't want the 42 million school children in this country to learn about ideas these people disagree with—everything from divorce to evolution."

In the non-jury trial before Judge Hand, the fundamentalists aired their complaints. Aaron Tabor testified that he was offended by the books he was forced to use as a student. Among other things, they seemed to say that taking the Lord's name in vain was all right. Aaron's father Byron maintained that his children were the butt of jokes in school because they believed in divine creation. Lynn Nobles objected to the philosophy of ethical relativism in the texts because it prevented her from teaching her pupils about absolute standards of right and wrong. Nurse Judy Whorton and her husband Robert pointed out that one social studies book failed to identify the Reverend Martin Luther King, Jr., "as a pastor of a church and never mentioned the role that religion played in the civil rights movement."

The plaintiff's position came down to this: The textbooks in question teach secular humanism. For all practical purposes, this set of beliefs is a religion. If the First Amendment prohibits the teaching of Christianity in the public schools, then it should also prohibit the teaching of humanism.

The defendant school commissioners replied that secular humanism is not a religion. And even if it were, there is no evidence that it is being taught in the challenged textbooks. Besides, the First Amendment does not prevent a state from using texts that include ideas contrary to someone else's religious beliefs. The commissioners admitted that some of the textbooks did a poor job of explaining the role of religion in American history. But the state superintendent would correct this problem.

On March 4, 1987, Judge Hand made his decision. He agreed with the plaintiffs' point of view and ordered the defendants to get rid of the forty-five history, social science, and home economics books.

He explained that the *Smith* case was different from the *Mozert* case. The Alabama plaintiffs wanted to protect their children from "systematic indoctrination" to secular humanism, whereas the Tennessee plaintiffs wanted to protect them from "mere exposure."

The judge considered humanism to be a religion because it meets these four tests:

- It makes a statement about supernatural existence.
- It defines the nature of man.
- It sets forth a goal or purpose for human existence.
- It defines the nature of the universe.

Finally, he concluded that the forty-five textbooks violated the plaintiffs' First Amendment rights in two ways. First, they promoted the religion of secular humanism. And second, they neglected Christianity to the extent that "a student learning . . . from them would not be [informed] of [important] facts about America's history."

Robert Skolrood said that Hand's decision "exposes humanism for what it really is—a wolf in sheep's clothing prowling through the corridors of our public education system, ravaging with [complete freedom] the character and quality of our schools." However, a spokesperson for PAW predicted that the judge's ruling would be overturned on appeal. In the meantime, said Anthony Podesta, the *Smith* precedent "gives fundamentalists a two-year supply of matches to remove what they disagree with."

Lastly, in Louisiana, the state legislature passed a law that required teachers to give Biblical "creation science" equal time with evolutionary theory. This statute resulted in a conflict between creationists and evolutionists. So the Louisiana case was more like the 1925 Scopes case and the 1968 *Epperson* case than other battles about specific school books.

On June 19, 1987, the U.S. Supreme Court declared the Louisiana "equal-time" law unconstitutional. The seven-to-two decision was considered a major setback for fundamentalists. Writing the majority opinion, Justice William J. Brennan, Jr., called the law a "sham." Its real purpose, he said, was not to give children a balanced understanding of life on earth but to advance one religious viewpoint to the exclusion of all others. However, Bruce Fein of the conservative Heritage Foundation replied that "the decision is a total assault on efforts to get anything related to religious [beliefs] into public schools."

The Christian fundamentalists, Citizens Organized for Better Schools, Concerned Women for America, National Legal Foundation, George Wallace, Pat Robertson, and the Gablers generally want to protect students from ideas that go against the literal interpretation of Christianity. Whether all the non-fundamentalists in the Tennessee, Alabama, and Louisiana cases think of themselves as secular humanists is doubtful. And it is hard to generalize about humanists as a group. Many, but not all, support the student's right to know. Some are liberals, others conservatives. Taken together, the final decisions in these three Southern cases will help define the legal relationship between fundamentalists and humanists throughout America.

Conclusion

I
n a 1984 article for *The New Yorker,* Frances FitzGerald identified "two previous waves of enthusiasm for book banning—one
in the nineteen-twenties and the other in the nineteen-fifties."
She also observed that "during the nineteen-seventies, an epidemic
of book banning broke out all over the country. . . . In a 1982 survey
of eight hundred and sixty school librarians, . . . thirty-four per cent
reported having had a book challenged by a parent or a community
that year." What made the "epidemic" of the seventies and eighties
different, FitzGerald maintained, was the opposition to it: "The one
clear novelty of the new censorship drive was the legal action taken
against it."

This study of recent school book battles agrees with
FitzGerald's observations. Many pressure groups felt the need to
protect students from possibly harmful ideas. These groups included Mel and Norma Gabler's Educational Research Analysts,

Christian fundamentalists, Concerned Citizens of Kanawha County, Christian-American Parents, People Who Care, Parents of New York–United, Citizens Organized for Better Schools, Concerned Women for America, the National Legal Foundation, and the Moral Majority. They backed individuals, families, and school officials who tried to prevent the purchase or use of books thought to be dangerous.

Many other pressure groups supported the student's right to know. They included the Presidents Council, the American Civil Liberties Union and its various state organizations, the Authors League of America, the Right to Read Defense Committee of Chelsea, the Church Hill Ministerial Association, Citizens Advocating the Right to Education, and People for the American Way. These groups—along with teachers', librarians', and publishers' organizations—also backed individuals, families, and school officials who tried to prevent the banning or removal of books.

Citizens who believe in the need to protect students have challenged an increasing number of school textbooks and library books in the past two decades. But citizens who support the right to know have won more major cases. Out of the nine main cases covered in this study, right-to-know groups have claimed victory in six.

In the *Minarcini, Right to Read,* and *Pico* decisions the Sixth Circuit Court, the Massachusetts District Court, and the United States Supreme Court ruled respectively that school boards do not have the authority to remove books from school libraries for personal social, political, or moral reasons. In the *Loewen* case the Mississippi District Court said that the state's authority to select or remove textbooks is limited by First Amendment rights of academic freedom. The Maine District Court in the *Sheck* decision gave high school libraries First Amendment protection. In the *Grove* case the

Ninth Circuit Court concluded that the First Amendment does not protect religious groups from being offended by what is taught in public schools. The West Virginia District Court came to the same conclusion in the *Williams* skirmish against the Kanawha County Board of Education. But, on the whole, the Kanawha County war was a draw.

Groups favoring the need to protect were successful in only two cases. In the *Presidents Council* case, the Second Circuit Court seemed to say that school boards do have the authority to remove books from school libraries. But the interpretation of this case has proved troublesome. Other courts disagree on its meaning. However, the Seventh Circuit Court in the *Zykan* decision clearly said that school boards do have the authority to select and remove books for personal social, political, or moral reasons.

Because of the number of challenges to school books during the seventies and eighties, some citizens believe that the need to protect has been overemphasized. But, as this study shows, the courts have supported the right to know more often than not. And the ruling in the *Pico* case is the main precedent on book censorship because it was handed down by the U.S. Supreme Court.

However, right-to-know advocates detect a shift in emphasis. When Ronald Reagan became President in 1981, he began filling vacancies in the federal courts—including the Supreme Court. Reagan's appointees tend to emphasize the need to protect. And the full impact of his appointments may not have been felt yet.

Also, right-to-know supporters won the *Pico* case by a slim one-vote margin. Different Supreme Court rulings in the Tennessee or Alabama conflicts could weaken the *Pico* precedent. And lower court judges may rely on the *Presidents Council* and *Zykan* decisions by distinguishing future cases from *Pico*.

But what disturbs all citizens concerned about quality education is the extent of self-censorship in American education today. Defending challenged publications takes time, trouble, and money. So there seem to be more words that writers fear to write, more ideas that teachers fear to teach, and more books that publishers fear to publish.

Paul C. Vitz is a psychology professor at New York University. He was a key witness for the fundamentalists in the "Scopes II" trial. Professor Vitz wrote a report called "Religion and Traditional Values in Public School Textbooks." Among other things, he accused publishers of censoring religious references out of elementary and high school books. The president of People for the American Way, Anthony T. Podesta, observed that "religion is simply not treated [in textbooks] as a significant element in American life." A PAW report showed that "left and right in the world of religion are ignored equally." And Steven P. Schafersman, president of the Texas Council for Science Education, criticized five textbooks for never using the word "evolution." He commented: "We can no longer hold Texas science education hostage to know-nothings and zealots."

Frances FitzGerald explained that educational publishers are simply "trying to produce something that will be bought and be acceptable." But various pressure groups may force editors to do some soul-searching about excluding all controversial material. And publishers themselves may have to reconsider the national effects of producing different texts for different states.

It's hard to imagine a democracy without pressure groups. Indeed, the nonviolent conflict between citizens is usually good for a democratic nation. The political tug of war often keeps the country from going too far in any one direction.

Problems occur when extremists try to censor another group's point of view completely. However, the Constitution is based on the belief that no single individual or group has a monopoly on the truth and that a free exchange of ideas opens the only real road to wisdom.

So the goal for citizens concerned about quality education today is to strike a reasonable balance between the need to protect and the right to know. But that goal is often difficult to achieve, especially in the midst of an emotionally charged school book dispute.

Certainly, parents have a need—even a duty—to protect their children from "harmful ideas." But that phrase must be defined and applied very carefully. "Harmful ideas" are not merely distasteful concepts or simply new views that contradict some adult's long-standing beliefs.

Literally, "harmful ideas" are ideas that cause harm, that result in observable, anti-social acts. A classic example is racism—a set of ideas that has clearly resulted in discrimination, injury, and death throughout the world. But the connection between the idea and the harm should be definite before censorship comes into play.

Requiring parental permission for the withdrawl of controversial school library books may be proper in some cases. But this policy raises basic questions about the whole purpose of education. Should children be taught to agree with their parents on every issue? Or, in a society that values individualism, should children be encouraged to form their own opinions? In other words, a restricted-access policy should be applied with great care and only after much public debate on the controversial books.

But even when citizens share the common goal of striking a reasonable balance, school book disputes are hard to resolve. Many factors have to be considered. Is the work under scrutiny a required classroom textbook, or is it an optional library book? How old are the students who use the material? Is the subject matter treated elsewhere in a more acceptable way? If the problem is the book's language, is that vocabulary essential to the author's message?

What are the motives of the pressure groups involved in the conflict?

The First Amendment to the Constitution protects individual rights of speech, press, worship, and assembly. This constitutional protection implies that Americans have developed different points of view on such emotional subjects as religion, politics, and education. Extremists who try to censor another group's point of view completely take the country too far in one direction. To restore the balance, individual citizens must have the courage to keep America safe for diversity—for the free expression of a variety of ideas.

Of course, as human beings, we will seldom find a perfect balance between the need to protect and the right to know. The golden mean will often exceed our grasp. But, whether we emphasize protection or knowledge, let us all strive for the wisdom to respect points of view that differ from our own.

Sources

The following major sources are listed in the order in which topics discussed in them appear in this book.

INTRODUCTION

Bryson, Joseph E., and Elizabeth W. Detty. *The Legal Aspects of Censorship of Public School Library and Instructional Materials.* Charlottesville, Va.: The Michie Company, 1982.

Epperson v. Arkansas, 393 U.S. 97, 89 S. Ct. 266 (1968).

Haight, Anne Lyon, and Chandler B. Grannis. *Banned Books.* New York: R. R. Bowker Company, 1978.

Nelson, Jack, and Gene Roberts, Jr. *The Censors and the Schools.* Boston: Little, Brown and Company, 1963.

Publishers Weekly. "Protest Groups Exert Strong Impact." 216:42,44 (Oct. 29, 1979).

CHAPTER 1

Book Review Digest. "Thomas, Piri." *Down These Mean Streets.* p. 1302 (1967).

Gerhardt, Lillian N. *Issues in Children's Book Selection.* New York: R. R. Bowker Company, 1973.

Newsletter on Intellectual Freedom. "Law Suit Challenges Book Banning by School Board." 20:81 (July 1971).

—— "Down These Mean Streets." 20:106 (Sept. 1971).

—— "Down These Mean Streets, Appeal." 21:136 (Sept. 1972).

Newsweek. "In the Arms of Lady Snow: Down These Mean Streets." 69:96A (May 29, 1967).

New York Times Book Review. "One Who Got Away: Down These Mean Streets." p. 1 and fol. pp. (May 21, 1967).

—— "Talk with Piri Thomas." pp. 45–47 (May 21, 1976).

Presidents Council, District 25 v. *Community School Board No. 25,* 457 F. 2nd 289 (2nd Cir.), *cert. denied,* 409 U.S. 998, 93 S. Ct. 308 (1972).

Snyder, Gerald S. *The Right to Be Informed.* New York: Julian Messner, 1978.

CHAPTER 2

Christianity Today. "West Virginia Uproar: Contesting the Textbooks." 19:44–46 (Oct. 11, 1974).

Commonweal. "Textbooks in the Hollows." 101:231–234 (Dec. 6, 1974).

Hefley, James C. *Are Textbooks Harming Your Children?* Milford, Mich.: Mott Media, 1979.

Jenkinson, Edward B. *Censors in the Classroom.* Carbondale, Ill.: Southern Illinois University Press, 1979.

Nation. "West Virginia Book War: A Confusion of Goals—Controversy in Kanawha County." 219:430-435 (Nov. 2, 1974).

National Education Association. *Inquiry Report: Kanawha County, West Virginia, A Textbook Study in Cultural Conflict.* Washington, D.C.: National Education Association, Teacher Rights Division, Feb. 1975.

New Republic. "Access Rights to Children's Minds: Texts for Our Times—Problems in Kanawha County, W. Va." 172:19–21 (Jan. 4, 1975).

Newsweek. "Book Banners: Kanawha County, W. Va." 84:94–95 (Sept. 30, 1974).

New Yorker. "U.S. Journal: Kanawha County, West Virginia—Anti-Textbook Controversy." 50:119–122 and fol. pp. (Sept. 30, 1974).

Time. "Battle of the Books: Kanawha County, W. Va." 104:81 (Sept. 30, 1974).

U.S. News & World Report. "Schoolbooks that Stirred up a Storm: Kanawha County Textbook Controversy—With Excerpts from Books." 77:61–62 (Nov. 4, 1974).

Williams v. *Board of Education of County of Kanawha,* 388 F. Supp. 93 (1975).

CHAPTER 3

Book Review Digest. "Heller, Joseph." *Catch-22.* pp. 534–535 (1962).

——— "Vonnegut, Kurt." *God Bless You, Mr. Rosewater.* p. 1295 (1965).

Contemporary Literary Criticism. "Heller, Joseph." 1:139–140 (1973).

——— "Vonnegut, Kurt, Jr." 1:347–348 (1973).

Current Biography. "Vonnegut, Kurt, Jr." pp. 429–432 (1970).

——— "Heller, Joseph." pp. 174–177 (1973).

Library Journal. "Ohio Court Bars Book Seizure by School Boards." 101:2120 (Oct. 15, 1976).

Minarcini v. *Strongsville City School District,* 384 F. Supp. 698 (N.D. Ohio 1974), *aff'd in part, rev'd in part,* 541 F. 2nd 577 (6th Cir. 1976).

Newsletter on Intellectual Freedom. "Students' Rights: Cleveland, Ohio." 23:18 (Jan. 1974).

——— "Students' Rights: Strongsville, Ohio." 23:152–153 (Nov. 1974).

O'Neil, Robert M. *Classrooms in the Crossfire.* Bloomington, Ind.: Indiana University Press, 1981.

CHAPTER 4

Publishers Weekly. "Massachusetts Judge Orders Banned Book to Be Returned to High School Library." 214:21 (July 31, 1978).

Right to Read Defense Committee of Chelsea v. *School Committee of the City of Chelsea,* 454 F. Supp. 703 (1978).

CHAPTER 5

Loewen v. *Turnipseed,* 488 F. Supp. 1138 (1980).

Newsweek. "A New View of Old Miss." 94:70 (Sept. 10, 1979).

CHAPTER 6

Book Review Digest. "Plath, Sylvia." *The Bell Jar.* pp. 1079–1080 (1971).
—— "Anonymous." *Go Ask Alice.* p. 490 (1972).
—— "Levin, Ira." *The Stepford Wives.* p. 781 (1972).
—— "Merriam, Eve." *Growing Up Female in America.* pp. 897–898 (1972).
Office for Intellectual Freedom, American Library Association. *Censorship Litigation and the Schools.* Chicago: American Library Association, 1983.
O'Neill, Terry, ed. *Censorship: Opposing Viewpoints.* St. Paul, Minn.: Greenhaven Press, 1985.
Phi Delta Kappan. "Clarifying Values Clarification: A Critique." 56:684–688 (June 1975).
—— "The *Zykan* Case: A Triumph for School Board Authority." 62:279 (Dec. 1980).
Publishers Weekly. "More Groups Join Court Action against Warsaw, Ind., Book Banning." 217:18 (May 30, 1980).
Saturday Review. "Book Burning in the Heartland." 6:24–26 and fol. pp. (July 21, 1975).
Zykan v. Warsaw Community School Corp., 631 F. 2nd 1300 (1980).

CHAPTER 7

Book Review Digest. "Glasser, Ronald J." *365 Days.* p. 500 (1971).
Contemporary Literary Criticism. "Glasser, Ronald J." 37:130–131 (1986).
New Yorker. "A Disagreement in Baileyville." 59:47–48 and fol. pp. (Jan. 16, 1984).
Northeast Magazine. "Banned in Baileyville." (June 27, 1982). Reprinted in Downs, Robert B., and Ralph E. McCoy, eds. *The First Freedom Today.* Chicago: American Library Association, 1984.
Publishers Weekly. "Soldiers' Language Causes Partial Banning of Vietnam Book in Maine High School." 220:16 (July 17, 1981).
—— "Judge Sends '365 Days' Back to School Library." 221:42 and fol. pp. (Feb. 12, 1982).
Sheck v. Baileyville, 530 F. Supp. 679 (1982).

CHAPTER 8

America. "Island Trees: No Decision." 147:24 (July 17, 1982).

Downs, Robert B., and Ralph E. McCoy, eds. *The First Freedom Today.* Chicago: American Library Association, 1984.

Library Journal. "Constitutionality of Book Ban Challenged by NYCLU." 102:530 and fol. pp. (Mar. 1, 1977).

Nation. "Banning Books: Decision in Island Trees Long Island Censorship Dispute." 229:390–391 (Oct. 27, 1979).

Newsweek. "Can Schools Ban Books?" 99:82 (Mar. 15, 1982).

Pico v. *Board of Education, Island Trees Union Free School District,* 474 F. Supp. 387 (E.D. New York 1979), 638 F. 2nd 404 (2nd Cir. 1980), 73 L. Ed. 2nd 435 (Supreme Court 1982).

Publishers Weekly. Various articles in 1976 and 1982.

CHAPTER 9

Book Review Digest. "Parks, Gordon." *The Learning Tree.* p. 785 (1963).

Civil Liberties. "Censors Read the Bill of Rights Wrong." p. 3 (Spring, 1985).

Current Biography. "Parks, Gordon." pp. 300–302 (1968).

Grove v. *Mead School District No. 354,* 753 F. 2nd 1528 (1985).

Newsletter on Intellectual Freedom. "Spokane County, Washington." 29:75 (July 1980).

——— "Intellectual Freedom in the '80s: The Impact of Conservatism." 30:174 (Nov. 1981).

——— "Mead, Washington." 31:212 (Nov. 1982).

——— "Mead, Washington." 34:85 (May 1985).

New York Times Book Review. "Witness to a Killing" (review of *The Learning Tree).* p. 4 (Sept. 15, 1963).

Time. "A Kind of Kansas" (review of *The Learning Tree).* 93:86 (Sept. 6, 1963).

POSTSCRIPT

Christian Century. " 'Scopes Trial II': A Narrow God Defended." 103:667–678 (July 30–August 6, 1986).

Mozert v. *Hawkins County Public Schools,* 579 F. Supp. 1051 (Feb. 24, 1984), "Memorandum Regarding Stories on Issue of Salvation" (Mar. 12, 1984), 582 F. Supp. 201 (Mar. 15, 1984). "Memorandum and Orders" (Dec. 18, 1986).

Mozert v. *Hawkins County Public Schools,* No. 84-5317, in the United States Court of Appeals for the Sixth Circuit (June 18, 1985).

Mozert v. Hawkins County Public Schools, No. Civ-2-83-401, in the United States District Court for the Eastern District of Tennessee, Northeastern Division (Oct. 24, 1986).

National Coalition Against Censorship. *Books on Trial: A Survey of Recent Cases.* New York: National Coalition Against Censorship, Dec. 1985.

Newsweek. "A Reprise of Scopes." 108:18–20 (July 28, 1986).

———— "Secular Humanism in the Dock." 108:96 (Oct. 27, 1986).

Smith v. *Board of School Commissioners*, Civil Action. No. 82-0544-BH, in the United States District Court for the Southern District of Alabama, Southern Division (Mar. 4, 1987).

Time. "Tilting at 'Secular Humanism.' " 128:68 (July 28, 1986).

———— "A Courtroom Clash over Textbooks." 128:94 (Oct. 27, 1986).

———— "Religious Bias." 129:66 (Mar. 16, 1987).

U.S. News & World Report. "A Bombshell Court Ruling in Tennessee." 101:8 (Nov. 3, 1986).

GENERAL SOURCES

Berninghausen, David K. *The Flight from Reason: Essays on Intellectual Freedom in the Academy, the Press, and the Library.* Chicago: American Library Association, 1975.

Clor, Harry M. *Obscenity and Public Morality: Censorship in a Liberal Society.* Chicago: University of Chicago Press, 1985.

Copp, David, and Susan Wendell, eds. *Pornography and Censorship.* Buffalo, N.Y.: Prometheus Books, 1982.

Davis, James E., ed. *Dealing with Censorship.* Urbana, Ill.: National Council of Teachers of English, 1979.

Hart, Harold H. *Censorship: For and Against.* New York: Hart Publishing Company, Inc. 1971.

Hurwitz, Leon. *Historical Dictionary of Censorship in the United States.* Westport, Conn.: Greenwood Press, 1985.

Kilpatrick, James. J. *The Smut Peddlers.* Westport, Conn.: Greenwood Press, 1973.

Lewis, Felice F. *Literature, Obscenity, and Law.* Carbondale, Ill.: Southern Illinois University Press, 1978.

Oboler, Eli M., ed. *Censorship and Education.* New York: The H. W. Wilson Company, 1981.

Thomas, Cal. *Book Burning.* Westchester, Ill.: Crossway Books, 1983.

Woods, L. B. *A Decade of Censorship in America: The Threat to Classrooms and Libraries, 1966–1975.* Metuchen, N. J.: The Scarecrow Press, Inc. 1979.

Woodworth, Mary L., ed. *The Young Adult and Intellectual Freedom.* Madison, Wis.: Publications Committee, Library School, University of Wisconsin, 1977.

Index

About the Author

Donald J. Rogers is a freelance writer and the author of *Press versus Goverment.* He graduated from the University of Notre Dame and holds a master's degree in American Studies. He has taught high school social studies and has worked as a social studies textbook editor. He is a member of the American Society of Journalists and Authors. Mr. Rogers' complete biographical profile can be found in the 1988 edition of *Who's Who in U.S. Writers, Editors & Poets.*